A LITTLE MORE RED SUN ON THE HUMAN

D1567702

BOOKS BY GILLIAN CONOLEY

Peace
The Plot Genie
Profane Halo
Lovers In The Used World
Beckon
Tall Stranger
Some Gangster Pain

CHAPBOOKS

Preparing One's Conciousness For The Avatar
Sinking Into The Leopard Pillow
Experiments In Patience
an oh   a sky   a fabric   an undertow
Fatherless Afternoon
Woman Speaking Inside Film Noir

TRANSLATIONS

Thousand Times Broken: Three Books By Henri Michaux
On Feeble Love & Bitter Love: Dada Manifesto By Tristan Tzara

PUBLICATIONS EDITED

Volt

A Little More
Red Sun on
the Human

NEW AND SELECTED POEMS

Gillian Conoley

NIGHTBOAT BOOKS
NEW YORK

ISBN 978-1-64362-011-4

Design and typesetting by adam b. bohannon

Text set in Adobe Caslon

Cover Art: *Birch*. From the series *On the Viewing of Flowers and Trees*, painted 1922 by Hilma af Klint.

Cataloging-in-publication data is available from the Library of Congress

Nightboat Books

New York

www.nightboat.org

AUTHOR'S NOTE

In making a book of new and selected poems, I set out to make a new work, one with its own arc and trajectory. Poems from previous volumes, while sequential, are gathered outside of their original collections in newly titled sections. New poems appear in "Next," the seventh section. A list of poems from individual collections can be found in the notes page at book's end.

Grateful and appreciative acknowledgment is made to all original publishers and editors of books from which these poems were selected: Rusty Morrison and Ken Keegan of Omnidawn Publishing; Joshua Beckman and Matthew Zapruder of Wave Books; and Gerald Costanzo of Carnegie Mellon University Press. With gratitude for the editors and publishers of literary magazines where many of these poems first appeared. With special thanks to Kazim Ali, Stephen Motika, Lindsey Boldt, Andrea Abi-Karam, Caelan Ernest Nardone, Brian Teare, Domenic Stansberry, Hawley Hussey, Love Nance, Curby Conoley, Billie Tom Conoley, and Gillis Conoley. To all the poets, friends, artists, students, teachers, singers, dancers, listeners and guides, this book is for you.

for Domenic
for Gillis

CONTENTS

. . . both necessity and contingency, those two crosses
of Western thought, have disappeared from the *post
iudicium* world . . . after the judgment, animals, plants,
things, all the elements and creatures of the world . . .
would then enjoy an incorruptible fallenness—
above them floats something like a profane halo.

GIORGIO AGAMBEN

I.
THE INVENTION OF TEXAS

The Invention of Texas

The sea left this place
to fend for its own water,
leaving prickly wind
and one yellow color.

Birth continued.
Coyotes sang to cyclones on the lope,
men chattered in caves
in a kind of scat orchestration.

Someone invented the wheel.
This begat a misunderstanding
of circles. The Indians looked askance and blew
hollow smoke. Mexicans slept in

circumferences of corn
(in fact were the first to see corn as curio).
Soon they began to stay up all night
watching the stalks,
mistrusting the green dance.

The white man,
whose spherical countenance
was at first viewed as incomplete moon,
beat everyone up,
lassoed the stars and rode amuck,
spilling trails of sequins.

The Ancestors Speak

The shoes we left empty filled
With your talk of trouble
And the loud surf in your ear.

We are the great gang
Of men and women
Sought though untried.

Dark-suited, unconfirmed,
We are your fatted cells,
Your hot blood and bruise.

You are our modern zygote.
Our divisible egg upright
At the crossroads

Where a girl lingers with a carnation.
If whatever ends with beginning
By ending begins, help our story

Take hold. We'll strut our whole selves
Inside you, stomp our sentence
In your mouth.

Bear us malice,
And you'll blacken the old tree.
The town's not the same.

We can't hold up
The one who falls.
Go willingly to the common deep.

Dare

In this town there is a long rope.
Discordant leaf-melodies
above a line of boys naked and lawless.

When they swing, they pass
their mother's good sons
walking drenched in holy water.

Each time the river sags
a little, invisibly,
winks to next in line.

The hemp flies back
wet and oily,
cold as their dripping fists.

Too often
they have felt lonely
without clothes,

but when they let go
they are like newborns
bending their blue knees,

their cry
not of the living
or dead, but the narrow between.

Woman Speaking Inside Film Noir

What I want happens
not when the man leaning on a lamppost
stares up to my room and I meet his gaze
through the blinds, but in the moment after,
in the neon's pulse, when his cigarette
glows in the rain like a siren
and he looks away.

I go back to bed and imagine
the sound of his shoes
on the wooden stairs, flight
after flight, my pincurls loosening,
falling across the pillow
gentle as dropped bolts of bargain silk.

When the door flies open there's nothing
but the translucent band of the radio,
still he steps toward me
in a pyramid of light.
Our shadows yearn across the dresser,
my perfume bottles glisten
like shots of scotch. The mirror
is one more stilled moon
that wants the wish of him,
his face upturned,
astonished, cloudy as opal.

Some Gangster Pain

Eunice is tired of pain, everyone else's.
She wants some gangster pain,
to strut her thick ivories
in a collision of dreams, the pajamas-to-work
dream, the magnolia siege dream.

What ya got there, Eunice, say Johnny and the boys.
Eunice lives behind the bus,
another fleeing place,
riot of exhaust. She doesn't
have much to say,
but she says it, hello.

When the boys talk
she feels her skirt
shift to the corner she took.
She sees them snap their fingers
to no dog. She knows

they wouldn't understand.
She knows her feet point themselves forward
but she keeps walking backwards in rain,
her heels too fast, or the rain seeps
into trees, she can't tell. She likes this street.

Johnny and the boys got on
jackets that twitch.
Eunice wears a lot of accessories. The boys
paint a circle on the wall
the color of lips.

Suddenly the Graves

I would never say anything against the dead.
I would drop my clothes to them
and say yes, see how the sun
won't leave alone
what we cover. My neighborhood
is startlingly radiant.
Yesterday yellow tanks steamshovelled
for the underworld. Otters dove
to sleek back their hair.
On the bench a man old as dirt
sat over his death
while teenagers, their hair
bright as planets, chased the greased
and iridescent ducks.

There is no peace in my mind anywhere.
If I nap in this light my grandparents rise
and mix their dominoes, their hands
rinsed of sun but bone-pure.
What if I left with them,
and shed my body? Would I
hear a single, melodious siren
singing the power,
the glory? Or would I
live on, as the earth continues,
in death's sediment, face to face,
these melodies strewn through me.

Tonight I Feel Mortal

Tonight I feel mortal,
like I could never grow another arm
the other two could love.

The important thing is to live winsomely backwards,
unbalm the decisions, good quick ones,
piquant decisions.

You have a theory:
Velcro on hips.
I have a storm glass window,

the possibility for refraction,
just letting the whole thing
refract. Hi,

here is my happy childhood.
I'll do my vigilante pop-up from the shell,
my hands cascading palominos.

You'll read this as a regional voodoo.
The house a vague tug
to cross the street,

I have painted my toenails red.
You have on shiny black shoes.
Our whereabouts are coming.

Premature Reincarnation

After your wordlessness, after loping
from fields that won't hide you,
bitter grass, colors
you lay down in,
for the last time
you will enter the trees, their music,
and crush leaves to your ear
as when you slept.

Every tree will wink in its complicity.
You'll see the rat
learn to fly
and the owl devoured. You'll run
to pastures your legs burn for,
a sky that can't take you
though you raise your arms.

There will be days of limit,
of indecipherable thought,
but soon your legs will straighten
and your arms tire and hang
so without reluctance
you will walk
into a house, discover
the hideous grass between your teeth,
darkened pads of your hands,
and work day and night
to remove them, to scrub and oil your body
though there is no flight.

You will dream
in a tamed language
you fear others can hear. In the day
in crowds of people or alone
at night in bed the curious will stir

within you, for you
have been struck
from the waters and the fields.
You are not wolf
or snake or hog,
and one day
you must rise without wings.

The Native

One day I looked
at the face in my shoes
and saw a way down the road
I was raised on.
Live in one town too long,
a lush plain
grows inside you.

Something of fields
that lie languid
beneath the moon,
dirt that disobeys
plowed rows
and lies at low levels
in the constant wind,

even the aluminum plant
moored in the distance, lit tall
like a ship just leaving,
can suggest a road
where before there was no road,
and a blessing.

On top the filling station
the cardinal's
red tomahawk
blinked off and on,
a drifter leaned on the gas pump,
and I headed out into the elsewhere.

To the highway I said
show me something new,
but it dove
forward and backward,
looped into unrestful heights
that turned into towns
where there were neighborhoods
I could not tell which
I was the shadow of,

so I drove on
in the many nights
among shiftless no-goods
walking sidewalks
with the ghosts of roses in their arms,
down the streets
that claimed my home
was invisible
and I never slept there,
that no town ever
stops talking to itself.

If you are still there,
Bubba Wilcox,
the girl you used to know
has run off
with my common sense
and is on her way
to your house.

Ask her in.
Give her something cold.

The Birth of a Nation

By 1915 gravity had begun to affect light,
and mass, to distort space
so that reaching the theater
was a struggle: couples faded between lampposts
until each came to a ticket booth
where a woman sat
under a lit dome like a huge moth
in the chlorophyll of her blonde hair.

Two dollars (twenty then) bought entrance to love
between a Southern colonel, a prison nurse.
Innocence was played by Lillian Gish,
rival of snow, the liberal senator's daughter
besieged in a cabin
by blacks in black face;
salvation, by a galloping wizard,
don of a mob of white-hooded white men.

In Washington, Woodrow Wilson emerged
from a theater moved,
saying to a handful of reporters,
"It felt like writing history
with lightning . . .
so terribly true." Our president began
to remove his spectacles, to maneuver
through the masses
tipping his hat, diminishing
into the night where Einstein slept little,

and the young Chaplin
practiced late,
falling again, again,
again onto his face.

The Singer

She wanted to walk, to stand upright
and not collapse
on the sidewalk like so many others
who had fallen in love with a man
who looked like a god
riding the horse
he had fallen in love with.

Midday, midnight. Such were
the substance of her songs,
and then silence, her lyre
like a broken arm.

Oh to give anything
for the moon like a sleeping pill
in the stuttering hotel sign,
blue as a barroom table
and as able to bleed.

To fold
the white napkins,
and not let anyone know
you're wounded.

Night into night she learns
to hold each note,
though the roads curl
like paper from her hair,
the rooms full of who and why
she chose the wrong nights

to stay out
late, at arm's length,
her feet stumbling
into a ring of sleep.

Like you she enters the melody
before it clicks shut.
Like you she surefooted
steps into herself,
past north, south, east or west,
her old child's eyes
written in red
like mad sonnets, this one
with her face to the cold,
and in front of strangers
she sings.

She sleeps alone against
shared walls, and wakes
to walk away, stage
by stage, bending songs
into the daily accident, miles
along the highway,
loving you.

Tall Stranger

Tamborine, violin, clouds
pursued to flame by sunset,
I needed something to distract
the sooty swallows,
something to help me face
the Pacific painting itself
in breakers, where I could walk
as into a movie and not pay.

In the desert the smell of things dying
turned flamboyant, the road
a path of fog. I was both
watched and watching,
balcony and tower,
in my head among clouds
I had the vulture's insomnia,
amnesia of the sky.

Then dance. Dance, they said
in the towns, bullets at my feet
so I'd be some ungainly marionette
dangling westward, eyes heavy with sight,
each town
a fallen bead of destiny.

I stumbled thirsty
to the smallest of towns
where there were more, more
miracles than I could fathom,
whole days of whoops and cries,

but in a store glass
when I finally saw myself
displayed among the sad treasures,
I had to know it was true
my life was broken.

A waitress,
the bride of no one
doused the last flame of the day
inside a café,
and tuned a TV past sand and haze
until my likeness appeared,
my lone being no larger
than human fate,
my dream her matinee.

My journey is longer than life,
my bewildered gestures
pulsed daily
from a shadow box
into the glassy bistros
atop the high silver beaks of banks.

When the sky drops its black chains
I rattle them.
I have a different fix on the stars,
and the frontier opens up again,
far into the interior.

The whole setting is abroad.
I could die out there.
I could live forever.

The One

Along the alleys I can hear the love songs
come out of jukeboxes like dying embers,
the songs played when lovers
walk away from each other speechless,
and the singer opens her mouth wide
to the scat that is the scandal
of the cross-languaged birds overhead.

Beneath that music, those birds,
in the stagger of my forming
I walk as though I have no hips,
as though when I sight proof of myself
my heart doesn't gallop,
nor my footsteps scald the snow.

Though the cinema is huge with me,
and murderers of my thoughts lurk
in the whole realm of possibility
that carries me like a mother,
I think I'm drifting off the icon stand,
I think I'm just another saint in a housedress.

Or the sparrow who nests low to the pond,
in love with her disturbing double,
because when I walk out of the love song
I fall in love too, like the pedestrian
waiting for the echo of my shoes to die down
as I step on the bus and hold the rail

like a captive, like a captive on a ribbon of road
stirred by the voices of travelers,
the cup I too hold in my throat atremble.

I don't know if this is life
or someone else's myth etched into my palm,
if this is wishful, or unutterable beauty,
but I have to drag my heel through the dust
then back off angrily
before returning to rain or night,
fatigue or hope for the lovers
who beseech into each other's arms

with my fate in their hands,
while in other rooms of smoke and lament,
professors turn blank pages,
looking for me.

Lee Harvey

Marquees, dim buildings,
crowds make me want
to forgive Oswald. Dallas
I have forgiven,
Dallas is a city anywhere
save for the red neon
Pegasus rising off Mobile Oil.

I have a cousin
looks a little
like Oswald,
though no one can
quite place him, no one
claims him on their side.

Sunday afternoons we'd go
to the Rialto
where technicolor Bible stories
washed over us.
When the screen went black
I'd touch his shoulder,

afraid that he was my cousin,
and he was never completely
anywhere. On the hot sidewalk home
he'd smile to himself
like he was in a silent film. I'd mimic
his pout, drop one shoulder

lower than the other.
Three steps to his stride,
in the childish rhythm
of my patent leather shoes
I fell behind to walk
with his shadow a slim partner.

The day was minute and vast and clear.
If I looked up I saw
glass and brick, if I looked back
I felt the family voice
in my throat, a mother's
nervous gesture in my hands,
a father's sidelong glance

and the sidewalk cracking
until there was the sensation
of rising off the ground, of walking
a little above the heat ghosts,
united with the power
of never doing anything alone.

Next morning my cousin
came down
in his one suit
and slung a pack of clothes
over his shoulder. He said
he was ready to confess

he had seen sparrows
writing messages
in broken hieroglyphs
to the president.

He had heard
the president laugh
in the wind.

When my cousin
walked out
the door burst into blue sky
and he joined the ranks
of unknown fellow men
walking between the country's
great towns, unpitying.
I grew up to live
all over
America. If the door flies open
and a road of light falls through it
I walk blind

to shut it back,
catching our features
before we turn,
smudged and darkly visible,
in the shivering pane. We throw out
our long shadows, our indivisible shadows,
then pull them in again.

Frontier Days

In the white morning haze
a town has when it remembers its former beauty,

donkeys stroll the desert floor,
an iguana trods the wide brown upland.

The incurious walk
brutally through last husks of summer,

like you should be lucky
to grow old at all.

The machinated bull
tilts and spins above stranger,

above friend, while over peaks
of the trembling tents

the sky rushes
herds of bison pushed by wind.

The deputy,
whose swagger was an era, descends

a stable nag, and ties a ribbon
to the white-faced cow.

Where is my country, someone asks,
in sleep, between blue ox and fantail hen.

The picture show exhales one huge stale sigh.
Down the street, under the elm, the lamppost light

aslant across the trunk's
knife-scars and dog-rubbed bark, is where

Joe Ray Moldenhaur got Carol Zimmerhaunzel
pregnant in the park. Their story expanded,

was spoken by so many mouths that no matter
how the words were shaped, they were not equal

to the salt and pitch
of the night that held them like a boat,

to the story that rose
half-woven to wind, vanishing,

connecting in 16 years
to the blurred velocity of the Moldenhaur boy

on a floodlit field, hurling a football
maybe not even 50 yards away, a hero,

his fully grown bones roaming beneath the flushed skin,
Carol and Joe huddled in the oncoming cold,

passing a silver flask of brandy
in the stands,

the elm's branches bare in the late fall dark,
and not an inch farther away.

Corn and live oaks move
as if God's page is being turned.

The white-faced cow
lows and grazes, her great head

suspending on the community her pale,
conscious animal lamp.

From craft tables,
creatures of killed pine,

the recipe voices of radio women
pipe down. On a makeshift stage the emcee

lowers his bullhorn,
and the last customer at the barbecue stand

quits repeating the simplest,
least intended things.

In the white scorch of a long white noon
where is my country, someone asks, in sleep,

between blue ox and fantail hen, the dream
of floating toward bursting stars

impossible to contain
our mixed blood in its prosaic channels,

the reversals, spaces,
retractions and galloping fantasies,

though you can still ask the dust
the blurry roadmaps of the district.

Cars whir lazily,
the sky exceeds its dome.

Breathless messengers
flow like oxygen,

and the roads curl back to Nowhere,
a town like any other

where we can live a while, towering,
an instant, in abundance,

singing hymns until again we are ordinary
boys and girls reciting,

our mouths stained with blackberries,
our hands over our hearts

in the spoil's ash,
in the stirred dust

leaping onto us,
and tasting of land,

its broken plainsong
our record of speech.

II.
DOUBT SETS IN

My Sister's Hand in Mine

Often without knowing how,
I would see you in a rain, in a hammock,
in a window, in yourself,
in a time more here than place,
like when you left the guitar
in the allure of a bus stop,
and pinned a tiny flag
to your dress. You remember.
There was a war on.
Men of a melancholy one could hold.
The past was a souvenir
that could propel us
from one void into another,
until we grew up
like women who sold perfume
walking around
in their dead aunt's shoes,
who walked an imagined land.
Our mother grew one dark,
particular rose.
A girl took a white dog walking.
We wanted more clouds, more iced tea,
more laughter that reached
into a pitch, that brimmed over
into intelligence.
Gradually there was a recital.
A certain Mary and Priscilla,
a psychopathic liar and a beautiful klepto,
a self that touches all edges.
It was an old saying torn

from a garden of birdbaths.
As children we were gawky.
What is beautiful? What is ugly?
What is Country? Liberty? Honor?

We returned home alone,
to improvise, on the piano.
The willow trees buried the willow trees.
It was like nothing you remember.
It was like how can you really
know anyone when beauty is as beauty does,
and the voice you thought was yours
seems to fly away behind you
like a ribbon caught in wind
chasing all that your story
was ever going to be,
while out of sheer pleasure
the streets unfold
into other streets.

Beckon

Dead cold spots in the air,
others bright and richly colored as opera,

my old dress is worn out,
torn up, dumped,

another thing the mad made.
Saddles laid out to dry,

vowels left up in the air as if something is better
left unsaid, as if I could have.

And truth is music's mute half,
a sentence broken into,

the half tone of a husband
waiting alone in a car,

so that only the sun warrants a red mane.
A figure passes quickly

in the ever-unquiet breath
of you, you, you and sometimes me.

The future nude, an absolute night
troubled by how we will live up

to the day's sequence of images in full sail,
as wind folds other things,

and ink branches and conceives.
Last night was floral,

a satin comforter fell
into violence, old

strangely beautiful voices
in the thin thread of my dreams

in the thin thread of my speech.
I was embarrassed because I wanted more lines near my eyes

and the laughter that forms them
to bring me luck's child.

I had a dream like seconal, sleepy rule of birth,
odor of seduction. I had only prayer, prayer

and science. On a street young girls gathered,
loud with nothing to say, as in an attempt to explain a local fire.

Standing Still Like Walking, Walking Like Standing Still

Everything disorderly and melancholy.
Everything massive and tall, or broad and wide.
The china stove enameled in blue flowers.
The beds so high, so rumpled, so devastated.
Once a mother in her garb and manner.
Once a father in his smoke and silence.
Their love. And then like anyone
struck by chance and affection, dust, dust, white bride
on the streetcar shuttering by.
My God, why hast Thou forsaken me
if Thou knew'st I was not God,
if thou knew'st that I was weak?
And going out in the natural night without enchantment.
Along the red trails, the small hotels sleeping soundly. One by one,
and one can hear the habit breaking, in memory
the pond's surface stirred, sky
pouring down into the sunken
garden, shaken. And all that begins to accompany you
dangling in the rhythm of your walking.
So that soon it becomes necessary to both
cultivate and tame, to learn to read what you see
and be patient there
(where time opens), embarrassed yet tactical,
balancing light and shade for those who cannot bear
to be around such aliveness.

So the wine stain in the drunken towel,
so the wondering of should I go to a movie?
And the screen's own erotica, the gels and lenses and washes
providing a limit as to how far to go

as we take the pleasure in. The pool's vacuum
cleans the littered surface,
silently, the white absence, the white anguish.
People wake and stretch and come forward, each seeing
how we want to go on,
without anybody's
getting hurt, one recalling meeting another
in a dark dream or was it April.

A voice trills at the end of a narrow, quiet street.
One remembers a lover's eyes, a lover's nose and chin
and the feeling of being
betrothed in the lax rich wind. Each a mound
that means a body, that wears a self
taking a path
of where we would be if we were here,
in memory's teasing outline, my love.

Doubt Sets In

On a leafy street whose name is gone

I hoped to manage

A brilliant black wax

A freeway lined with oleander

But doubt set in as if trying to express

A color in the paper

My motorcycle spinning past

Plants subject to metamorphosis

Hedges of privet, shivering palm

The vulva of an iris

A suitcase in the desert

Our neighborhood prepared for carnage and riot

In what language bitter and imprecise

As an old tombstone rubbing did we spawn

Terrible, terrible youth and the heart empty

Since the hate crime

No loss softened by that free museum

Others calling in the warm night

Beside an expansive sea hiked up like a skirt

On the courthouse steps as the bride frees her white balloon

I practice stillness, addressing the heavens

72 degrees, beautiful season that is not all appearances

Taking a white curve on a dusty blackboard we call logic

I wonder if we are fixated here

On kindness, vast domain where the frontiers are

Committing the world to memory

No atom feels, no heaven comprehends

Just wanting a motorcycle ride on a warm day

Out on the great meadows before spoken things

The world awash on its shaky brilliant legs

Doubt sets in like the confident gait of an armed child

Lamentation for Martha Graham

On a country porch a traveler in shadow
brings such a darkness you could marry

one summer night's lament with a mild wind,
refrain to refrain. Follow the path to lyric,

and a movement never lies,
a fate gathers shape, Noguchi's metal dress.

Bead your lashes with a wax candle,
compose a face

human and flawed like art out of nothing
and try to live forever

though they'll cut you in two,
the river and the moon.

Walk alone through time, each movement
the ruth of a summer gale,

a wind turning through a red farmhouse
flush with cloud, Appalachia,

cold air of the white camellia,
dawn's human gait.

On the frontier a woman fell backwards
in a black evening gown,

her sinewy waist an enemy of snow.
Leaving an expanse so wide, sweet audience,

we did not want the night to end.
We did not want to leave the building.

Dorothea Lange

All of consciousness is shifted from the imagined,
the revisive, to the effort to perceive simply the cruel
radiance of what is . . . This is why the camera seems to me,
next to unassisted and weaponless consciousness, the central
instrument of our time . . . If I could do it I'd do no writing
here at all. It would be photographs.

JAMES AGEE

Work pants, housedress, long underwear draped between pines. Dandelions drying in the
pickle jar. Wildflowers in loose cement. Seek and thou shall find. The rough, the hewn,
words spent as in only enough water to wash the clothes, not feed the land. Worst thing we
did was sell the car, but we had to sell it to eat, and now we can't get away from here. Cast
iron pan roped to the rear of the Ford. Free AIR for Tires this is YOUR Country Don't let
the big men take it away FROM YOU. When it snowed last April we had to burn beans
to keep warm. You can't get no relief until you've lived here a year. This county's a hard
county. They won't help bury you here. If you die, you're dead, that's all. Next Time Try The
Train, Relax. White Angel Breadline. Near the mounds where fire ants burrow. On the
sidewalk's heat-buckled steps. A girl sticks her tongue out to make another girl turn away.
Chilled, dawn, a woman wanders toward the station. As her hair fails. Mended stockings
pooled in espadrilles, the woman draws the black line up her calf.

From interviews with assistants we
learn that although Lange was aware that
photographing these people might eventu-
ally help them, she did not allow herself or
those with her to offer money or equipment
to help those so clearly in need. Lange
recognized that she was in a position of
privilege, a status conveyed by clothes,
class, and government support. One way to
relate to the migrants in a seemingly more

equal way was to win their sympathy, lessen
the differences between them.

But it did not sufficiently benefit
Florence Thompson, the unnamed subject of
"Migrant Mother." For her, the appropria-
tion of her face, in what came to be regarded
as the "art" of the Farm Security Adminis-
tration, and her "story" was a matter she
wanted to be recognized by cash payment, as
she assumed that Lange was made rich by
the photograph. Only when Thompson's
children (pictured in the famous photograph)
and her grandchildren, then comfortable
San Fernando Valley residents, were in-
terviewed in the 1980s did they reveal that
they enjoyed their place in history as
documentary "art" of the 1930s.

—Curious that as I go through, how many of these things that I count as great seeing
are things I made on the edges of something else that I just see at the end of a roll, or
far away, badly exposed, not part of the main-stream, but those things . . .

—A piece of meat in the house would like to scare these children of mine to death.

—We'd like to starve if it hadn't been for what my sister in Enid sent me.

*   *   *

Storefront glass
    silvers the view.
A group of men
       standing in line shove up
against the picture plane.
       Do we go inside, or do we let it blow over?

Fallen clapboard,
    barely a girl
        sleeping on her bed
of crushed briar.

Gone far enough West,
    a bartender wipes down
another glass
    as if he'd seen himself do it.

*   *   *

In the Home of the Depraved
in the Station of Newly Arrived
who is
a shepherd. What is
the maker.
Dust over the body
bent over dust on the plate.

Leica in the glove compartment
she drove her rental car away and into.

Salt down her neck.
Clavicle.
Cracked vinyl.

As in to sit.
Unassisted.
Weaponless.
Only what's there, there.

Heroes, Saints, and Neighbors

X was a common hood.
Taps on his shoes,
what he meant by that, syncopation
down the hall,
crop dust in his wake.
He wanted love and denial,
frequent and percussive,
the sunburnt evening out of town,
the beginning of a word
an expectation, the maple red ice birch,
can of Skoal in his rear pocket.
At the grocery, the woman swings her arm out
to get a look at her watch, and an old woman
in hat and gloves, cane at a jaunty angle,
looks out the timed doors, watches the local flag snap.
In the end nothing a settled thing to have experienced.
Miscreant government, cold hands portend
a shiver over the grave.
We perform a common language, a harp played
by its errant strands, a harp on fire
on an island no one can remember
one solid thing about.
Gulls sweep the glassy wave before it crashes.
A toddler tumbles onto sand.
Downtown buildings all come together
to the hypotenuse
in a myopia stronger than nationalism.
All kinds leave the pool hall,
rhapsodic minute discriminations
opening like snapdragons,

sunlight a bronze armor bound by the season.
We are not a beautiful people.
We are the kind you find dreaming and walking
city streets at dawn, out at the edge
where there is no I or not I,
avoiding the horoscope. No great epigrams
issue forth from us, no thin tigers
prowling, out to earn even more stripes,
no roses on our lapels the way spies
find each other. Consider long the face
of the person next to you: mouth open,
stray sheet mark, hair
obvious on the skin. Look
for the spirit that hides in the face,
that sinks into deep, marvelous sleeps in the afternoon.
Let others blur the balconies with silk.
A woman, a man lights the desk lamp in the lobby,
then walks into the bar and touches the piano.
High in a hotel a stray hand
surveys the blue radio dial,
and down the dim hallway you can never
find out what happens
to most people. Music is expectant,
a lipsticked cigarette, a pink invoice,
a book shorn of its cover.
A broom or a saxophone pierces the highest marrow of sound,
a capture, a release
we believe, we believe all our separate lives,
people framed for an instant by windows,
the colors wet, clear,
common, no dream coming up to the original.

Whose Nocturne

Uneven, internal, asymmetrical,
additive, color the chill steals from the peach and the apricot—

mothers heat the soup,
strangers to the girls they were,

low trees catching all the moisture.
A metal spoon, a rung chair, the cabinet's

chrome pulls—Headlights flare
against the wall and frame us,

my mother head turned down into the face of the beloved,
and just learning to live

in that instance,
in fate. Loose substance of matter,

faint hoot of the gutter owl
and the stars flake.

Our new faces tired
and divided by mercy in reds,

yellow beams, black
of the pupils receding to hold

the story and its undoing—the she and the I
and our collision—The first light

coming to betray us,
bestirred as the city's low hum,

hiss of the J-train,
the cry of its several brakes—

(and the body, never to feel "itself anymore")

dissolves into the dusk and the voice.

All Girlhood Receding

In the room I remember the wallpaper,
the stricken beauty, the bloodrag, the floral suitcase.

And all the brief anxious souls
surfacing, wanting in.

With each raking wave down the spine, with every *girl, girl,*
pick, hammer, drum

chafed like a lover.
And how hollow of knee, armpit, ankle—

how little my body
had anything to do

with me. Finally struggling
from the bed one woman casting the others

(the surly girl, the patient madam)
aside. It was she

who opened the door
(I remember her sinewy arms, her half-heard demands)

as she bore in the void,
the window a theater of cruelty,

fine line of the horizon
blind with noon on the streetcar's track,

the blurred portal
where the woman and the man looked back, through

to the girl and the boy they were, girl,
boy, who were they—

The Birth

You and I have our call and response,
we have a lyric at work not at rest,

the words torn and fleeing,
white sky, word blood in the day bed
until there is no longer a name for us.

Only souls who are dead,
young ones who are missing, the completely transformed,
so many faces, so many cheeks,
eyes, so many gradations of irises in the eyes

as a soul rushes, as the sun presses
and the heartless muscles urge further
down the slowly unraveling crimson rope
where each name pales, longing,

and the body—no longer yours, not mine—
pushes into the cold linen stunned light and just the

abyss, what is it, that sent no death—
only silence, breath,
the voice that cries
falls between us and we find

the way to each other—

The Big Picture

The ocean is dark blue, the blue sky is pale next to it,
the sun over-oranged as a Cimabue or a juice,

the palms new and vibrating, still tied up in hairstyle
even more than we who have come here by dint of passion and money

to the city, to the hair, clothes, lips and skin,
for the sweet butter, for the pleasure trousers, for the olive bird,

for the memory,
to take the hotel and lie in bed

with TV with blowsy curtains in the blue light,
the silent trains, the black trains, history's corpses

shuttling in
beside the terrific presence of your body—

A woman discovering a product,
a man standing motionless outside the project,

the idea of beauty and of a human nature perfect on all its sides
are what I can remember

about a childhood, a pudding,
an evening of tall grass.

Temporal, carnal,
I was a lazy teen,

I loved the slow film of a dress,
(a compass, a noise in the grass)

and in confusion, eloquence,
recurrence, eventually

next to my skin lay my dead aunt's pearls,
the beautiful factory where my slang was alive—

In the vestibule
of the brief shard,

burritos and limes,
on the giant screen swum the scattered elements of a violent beauty,

and I learned to love what was there like a child.

3/3/91   4/29/92

The sun sticks its head in the ocean.
God is and God dies,
and the night becomes as intimate as a little mall.

A bus noses down
narrow streets, summer greets us
cooly from a screen. The same sparrows as yesterday

start to wake in the disheveled wigs of the royal palms,
in a melody all
broken wings and artificial flowers.

A sparrow bathes in a puddle,
in ashes, slow, hesitant, like a small nation's
unconfident leader, and despair

won't turn into rapture,
it persists. Where speeches end, a madman
faces a dark canvas

as he would the face of a beloved, and begins
to mutter
in a versatile, alien language

pure as music
something about the new clarity.
Our children break the mirror with an axe.

Whites beat a black to death,
blacks beat a white to death,
only no one dies.

Behind curtains the protected
stretch out still
upon the silken red divan. The epoch won't end,

the heart beats and is beaten, smoke
follows lightly as the breath of a sleeper,
and the dawn is hoary with dew.

After

The composition was ready.
In the finished garden the corn and basil, fragrances mixing

in the humid chlorophyll,
the shaved grass full of dots and cells

as under a microscope. You slept backwards
that night, death in the portraits,

death in the tea,
death in the French doors—

As if you could get him back that way,
or follow along his bardo—

Only you were still breathing in the house of flowers,
the lilacs at their time of perfection, pining visibly—

And a man was traveling,
giving swell to the cloud

among people whose souls were already mature,
among those who were just forming,

while you found there was no way out of here,
some street to flee down, some room on the top floor to hide in,

and as though without strength
or the means to venture

(the mockingbird, the grackle in tatters
and their *caw, caw* at the trash men lifting a branch)

stepped among what
he had left . . .

Sandals on the deck,
                    the persistence in matter—

We Don't Have to Share a Fate

We don't have to share a fate,
we don't have to draw shameful conclusions.

After the shutter releases,
I want you in the multiple,

in the glacial carriage,
in the snake cloister,

in the closet full
of guitars and stomped hay,

in the exhalation of others,
all swaying with love, but changing midway

through the words
I address to you, my hand

pressed to yours visibly
much paler

than before, an orchid
offered beneath a warring sky,

an orchid that yawns
and cracks open and falls apart

unexpected in a bed of soft clothes,
where your shoulders became two steps,

dawns fruits rivers and knives,
full glottal, wide lens

and your hands became two countries,
and my legs murmured like grass,

a dumb love,
a tether to all dreams of enduring,

long convoy between two powers
killing the mockery of words

while daylight floats,
orchids, white dogs stretched out between the slow-burning lanterns.

Pale Sojourner

The sun rests deliberately on the rim of the sierra.
The raw rain falls,

the moon hangs over
love, brokenness, that which is not constant.

A woman
the central frozen image

the heart would break
standing on a corner in front of a drugstore,

particular out of the span
set into time and discarding time,

a voice fretted uneasily to music,
our sayings floating back

in the sky, traffic,
photographs, the grammar and the silence—

By what eternity are we invited,
flung shores, action painting, the traceries—

hearing a voice composed of notes
and stripped of certainty, talking,

whispering side to side,
close and yet offish in the distance,

a voice on the stair, a voice in the encyclopedia,
a voice of the kind in a barn

a child answers
when no one is there,

a voice that asks us to read
the titles to the right of the paintings,

sometimes just to look at the paintings themselves.
Among things said a voice that wants to know

are you still alive?
Are you broken?

Is there a lyric that is a mercy
there, a sky to call upon?

The words wager
against themselves

before responding
as to a siren. A voice

calls ahead, turning back
on the you and the I and she and he

as we do in a crowd,
remembering someone uncollected

in their splendor of this hair
and that shoulder and this head

passing among windows

of many years ago—in the white space

where our near and escaping souls
must be drifting

in lone personality and lost footing,
turning as we turn

to see our quick face
                parting, glancing—

III.
THE USED WORLD

The World

It was just a gas station. It was not spectacular carnage.

A woman in a parking lot, red I Love Lucy kerchief, dousing his shirts with lighter fluid,

a great love and a paranormal morning.

In the far fields the aliens arriving, switching off the ignition,

new crisp list of abductees   though the closest we get is the radio.

Cool gray summer morning the first heat making an aura.

Let light. She lights each panel. Fires twisting.

Whatever must seek out its partner and annihilate with it. A great love.

The expansion today is just a gas station. It is not spectacular carnage.

So one has a set of events from which one finds one can't escape

to reach a distant observer.   And a star is born.

Red giant, super giant, white dwarf.

We observe a large number of these white dwarf stars.

Giant Sirius, the brightest in the night sky,

dog star. What we could have been had not the star

been present, too much presence

seeping out of us—red the I Love Lucy kerchief draped over the lamp.

A she-ness to the table.   Pearls on the bread plate, make-up on the napkin,

a couple of burned-out butts.

(Alien intake valves?)

And come night: a supper club.

High risk behavior in cinemascopic rain.

The heat released in this reaction,

which is like, a controlled hydrogen bomb explosion,

which is like, what makes stars shine.

Boy Pegasus   Boy Mercury   Sister Venus

the stars so compulsively readable   the sun eight light minutes away,

Birthmark. At the red end of the spectrum.

Three gold-jacketed overly friendly men smiling,

poling before the nymph of a red river   burning in the presence of the floor plans.

For the world is one world now   not that you may own your own home.

Sinter me, sister.   Threescore skullduggery,   endless cradle holding a space open.

Rufous skylark,   tell us off the skiff,

sun up, the next day,   we're looking into a box.

Let's see the world.   Are you coming with me.   What's for dinner.

Several Skylines

The city adored the roadmap

the pencil taken from my hair
a mall of fireflies, a lakefront of white noise.

Money is

no final resting place
no closed down factory

lit in the supple way
everything measured tries looking.

The sky produces tender

colors down the aisles
each promise

blurred, the boxed

slogans and bright hands
arrested
in the glare—

My headlines mildewed in the storm.
The pipe bomb extant in the abandoned truck,
and in the big pain of not having
a million things, of being alone and with free time,

there was no landscape,

no one way
to walk the highway.

I'm going out now with a towel and a cooler for the river.

I start and error, and am protected by music.
Where the future shatters
a tiny office,
where a sister dyes her hair, and dyes her hair, to show what silence really is.

Canon

In the *as if, as if*   of storm into soaked leaves

the traffic's hiss

pantyhose on the clothes hanger

a personal life written on newsprint

an excellent acting out—

Later I deep-fried the catfish and let the grease drain.

On the screen's unwadded bedsheet,
the woman stabbed and the man running
about as long as a movie.
The moths born pile to hole in our towels.

As we put our books down

and took the stairs

and walked straight
to the stores,
                  as we made out shapes

with respect   in kind
in deliverance   in ardor

(anxious red wagon beside the moving library)

as we wished, as we said, as we gave birth or not,
it all got uttered,

again   again

until whether in scale or in patina,
we began to drift away from the conversation like thought,

your flourish,

my balm and plumb,

(who was that speaking)

We must remember everything,   *everything*

palm from infinity broken

Turned Back

So hot at the filling station

everyone moving like the not quite

utterly dead, a youth sucking on a mint, a toddler kicking a can of pop,

someone taking the key to the "john" taking obvious pleasure

in becoming another one

                  of the unlocated—

You can read the mystics/ you can lie down with the martyrs

and brood
on that other
as one would fade in a river

beside infant white

             foliage of the road

in the may-shine.

        Cloud's

thin amorphous plumage,

Daphne's singular girl peeking out from a tree
as time lags

        while the photos come back developed,

heavy beam of a head pressing down the frail summer leaves.

Inside the pumps the numbers rise,

and here a mind wanders here the fumes escape,   a youth walks out through the
noon.

Someone rushes around
the cash register

       hands smoothing the money
       like an attention span—

the silver drawer a site of purity

                      a zero aperture

                      a youth's cigarette

                      stabbed into tawny scratches

on the wall, someone's

            unspelled misery over a plot of marigolds—

The silver drawer lowering with the cash

           where you step forward

eye seeking eye in the pyramid,
in the paper oiled

in strip mall's
           blunt shadow cooling the back of your neck,

identity falling through the shaft
           before finding another house-a-fire for you,

                (and through
                the lively opening)

whose both ways close
with the silence of those

whose power can no longer enter anywhere,

                the sun in the present,

that fame—

someone flipping the radio putting voice over abyss

         someone folding a map

         someone bringing the sunglasses back down.

The Sky Drank In

The sky drank in   sparrows making lucid the oaks.   The leaves sank onto the stair.

And you   as you were,   I as I become,   color and form, bend and start,   split one

on the other side of *the screen of*   *your projections*—

you wanted me.   But I wasn't around,   only a small soul asleep   in the high heel,

or fluttering among the cosmetics   blindly, usually just a pause   between

what's there and not there,   mail on the stoop,   lists   "to do"

and other narcotics   we call beauty,   symmetry, harmony,

and no supplied thing—   Only a weak-edged soul,   the almost seen

luminous circle breaking   to parenthesis,   tender embrace   trying to enclose

whether for an instant or an eternity,   something is

"true—"   The sky   drank in sparrows making lucid the oaks.   Whirl

of particles in the desire of   whatever I sought   when I began

these sentences   (I stay,   I have stayed, I am staying),

the slow burning in of the come back   darling, the salesman,   the waitress,

the couple fighting in the phone booth   heart wall to heart wall, palm,   darkening lip,   the infinities that were, were

our mouths and our sex—   you who were not   becoming not once more—

lovers   in the used world,   more extinguished, finer

o you-again,   o one,   o no one,   o you—

The Violence

We must try to rid evil of our character, the president says.

The president is paling, another mouth of extinction, suggested the Fox.

I said over here, goddamn it, and not in the garage. I was
fourteen,

and learning to drive,
I knew the beloved must not be a monster in the head.

And so the world sins, it is exhausted, ministering to the misbegotten.

And so, shuttered in the subway, a murderer
rides between cars, so that he is before the wrong,
and the dead wrong, brother.

I was far from home. He held up a blank sign and I let him in the car. I did not want to
tarry.

My beloved is not
a monster in the head, my beloved is either
God's vengeance or his love,

entrails or insight,
I can only give you my word, though the fire in my eyes
is almost
his fire.

Genet: "A miracle is unclean: the peace I was searching for
          in the latrines and that I'm seeking
          in remembrance is a reassuring and silky peace."

Heraclitus: "Come in, there are Gods here, too.
              Don't be a stranger at the threshold."

In the tear of the pattern
no fleece shall cover you,
no seed-time, no unguent, no mystical birds, no eternal variant, gentian, algebraic,

no
eloquent
          alcohol, in the tear of the pattern,
no weed-grown

trail where a person could rest
in one
of a few mutilated copies—

Our no God sitting low on the other half of the tree, her shroud drawn over her hair–

Then take the cloth up again, the president says.

In the tear of the pattern, the wolf is whole, suggested the Fox.

And you are most vile.
You are a threshold spikily
gone through.

So this is your winter body, so this is your summer ass.

Sunlight glints over the breasts and the early evening newspaper, God's vengeance, or his love,

whose voice
so lightly   come of wounds

who loves   this way—

How Do I

How do I

How do I
count when it was another kind of verdancy
that brought me to you—

the ways not knowing otherwise
the trees weighted into a kind of prayerfulness
the wildflowers standing up against us, against being, against ideal Grace

so that we may forego symmetry

so that passion finds use
in we left to count when the breath
is not a grief and is not for counting

but is this repetition and this eternity

how I do, even
in most quiet need

discount ever
my unblinking glance my open face

how do I, in the tentative sun
that comes into

the nonfading
of the there we sat, there we were, after death.

The World

It is honest.

It is most unfair.

A day consisting wholly of noises.

Unsuspecting people shooting a playground with guns.
Never caused

any trouble before. I don't get it. No matter whether

I buy the orange one, or the magenta, or the chartreuse,
I've gone west, and I feel tranquil, not elated.

Cold wet girl squealing on her slip-n-slide,

slow river of hypodermics under a street lamp, anonymous deaths and not so asinine.

White, yellow, black,

a space preceding the image and a space following,

space and waste and shadow,
and Kilroy was   and Kilroy was

garnets under a radiation apron,

the quantum figures figured out
then crumpled up

and tucked
under your windshield.

Memory a kind of faceless Amish doll shivering me timbers, dancing in crushed shoes.

Where I come here, rounding the corner in my new speedster, and I ask you.

No, the landscape is not a collage.   It is wholly original.   My bare hands.

The Splendor Fragments

—

Between X and noon,
the blend of acids, sentiments, returning

weather which makes the night
transparent to think of—

like God's lonely imagination, and God's dark authority—

how for him
Death is the loving one, perfect for beating life into form.

—

"This way, please,"
was all she told me,

more her mouth   holding onto the words
than speaking,
       because no sound came out—
no melon patch on a summer's morn.

—

The words LIVE GIRLS torn
on the telephone pole, the earlier details
gone,

in country and in town.
Twilight. Forms
darkening,

how after the epidural
the hospital a shady white hotel.

—

A lonely rook strikes her beak
        against the white surface of the lake.

a pleasant drunkenness,
        a doubtful authorship.

—

In a climate of suspicion,
        fish fried, sheets hung,
                a rosebush

detonates,
        only what is in shadow

mattering
truly, eternally.

—

As when Genji's lover
 covers her mouth to laugh,
and the powder comes off in her hands.

—

In the mall's
vector of space

mannequins bent at the knees
        open eyes of longing

I tried on this dress,
a false pregnancy.

—

Summers in underpants,
blue tangled shopping cart,
everyone out for the immersion—

like Stein
composing *Three Lives*
under that Cezanne—

Pretty soon—
pretty soon I caught the drift of God's speech

before I polarized
completely.

Doggy in a window:

little lamb   who   made   thee

———

First sunny day
                    after rain,
my eyes just touched by the blue—

Visibility's   candidate, the mass marketers
enter me into their new computer,
                    I wander freely

amid cars parked sideways
in brilliant rooms—

———

Eternity flattens. And opens,

like sitting alone for a moment in a café
in a hole in the wall in the sorry chair in the middle of the dirt of the place,

then the urge to take that look off your face,
get the particular hell home.

———

The obduracy of spirit,
the loathing of self,
and the night, very fast—
on the overpass on our way to your house
I'm thinking new lover how well you speak my language

      taking the exit as we move beyond
the new sign,

but blank this time—

            the saying coming down the road
            on a truck somewhere

            like a little white bible in the human mind

            all that absence of being on the freeway

      through the portholes (false manor) my hand grazes yours

            a fool flies

—

Above moving sidewalks,
in shrinking headspace, pressed

among others,
unboundaried hair skin familiar to the touch,

I caught a movement of God's
lips, begging the question,
but he wouldn't
speak—   you don't   love me?

—

My waterloo, my diorama,

A white cypress

stretches

a fair hand.

Interior sea,

smooth urban lake,

all its runners
                drunk on fresh air
and syncopating their legs

left, right, breath,   no breath,

where shafts of the sun had fallen,

or as far as what's seen

(will stay)

Childhood Home, a Panorama

A crow on the telephone pole, tingeing daylight.

A television
in daylight
is a clear cosmetic bag,

is a transformation and a recreation,

a water in the inner ear.
A black woman is lowered
on a creaky Otis elevator—

originally designed for polio victims in the home—

a vacuum cleaner's hose wrapped around one ankle,
she raised me. I love her.

Will you pour me a sidewalk? she asks.

My sister a stripe of white above her black eyeliner
turning over out of her sunbath.

Surely a murder, surely a murder
places itself deep center, in the kitchen, in the hallway,

in the myrtle, in the purple vitex,
in the laughing that took you up tearing mint for the tea.

A Japanese soldier's sword hanging over the mantel,
sea pearls encrusted on the blood-splattered handle,

with no sense to the story at all,

like the sense of shape in a bowl of farm eggs,
their barely connecting

peripheries of humor.

Are you a handler, a healer, or an eater?

The eyes of strangers come to town in the right conditions
refracting red

in sulphur glow and pitchlight, the rattlesnakes obey
men without shirts,

silver buckles glinting over their blackened jeans.

Hot spectra
filling the falling summer sky,

somehow equivalent to leaving the next day without a trace.

In a loose white housedress a neighbor walks to the same crack
in the sidewalk every afternoon, and back. Cipher that.

As a practice I find it to be almost insatiable.

In the distance the lamentation of the train,
the lamentation of things no longer important.

What kind of facts began to hang in your brain?

Oxygenation, a mindful weather in the kitchen, half a melon.

The beds in their disheveled beauty.
Ever-biding sun.

We are glorious, but grow
in the awful knowledge that governors and heroes
rise in houses such as these.

A plaque that could say,
a plaque that could one day say a little history
to make you stop.

My sister handing me a training bra.   My sister's eyes a hazel green.

On the side porch all the men I will ever kiss.
But not the women, and not the children.

No matter what. I will swear I didn't do it.

It's hot, it's hot, it's hot.

The First Three Minutes

Deathless galaxies,
our beds,
unmade—

My sister reaching over me.
My sister going up in flames.

Our growstick
next to a tenuous mirror.

And like not the thing itself
but the culture that produced it, the thing opening.

All the future things   (we would make the car red,
        the guitar acoustic, a clear day
            would be one without membrane—)

shaking out like that,
        with no one around, the early convulsing—

The system becoming system,
before we knew it, dicey stars and a weak radio static,

time misfiring into the embarrassing moments before no theory
could take us to,

the black night in the black night

and where was the signature

and where was the mop against the door—

Lovers in the Used World

A luna moth
               in night's friable matter,

spun right into the image shadow, spun

behind time,
in the erstwhile Nowhere,

where silence
sends word

they are living over the difficulty: that what got lost in the mutations
was not what was

lost in mutability,

the leaves in comfort, the leaves in error,

in the channels of time spiralling
in spent time:

                     some rainy summer day with the sun out.

Her hair pinked, lifted
behind her, she is teasing myth's

trajectory in the sun-slatted tunnel where she can watch the heroines fly.

He is listing the summer words.

The *lucid* and *drowned* and *lost*,
and the "light" and the "fields" and the "huge"

and the thoughtful—

where they reach a space—
                    like brides come to be annointed

in a vatic streak—

A white, white interior—

Matter dropping into its sinkholes
matter blowing off the visible stars

the motes of dust authoring

who among us

who among us
would live more fatefully

and not in just what
chance arranges—

And without hunger
for the way images become one and beauty scans the eye,

and girls scrape
the rocks weaving.

How then are we borne up?

The great hand smoothing over
the great hand smoothing over,

                    and lifted from the fire.

Sapphic: I Said to My Instrument

Chapeau in sky before the photographer

Bringing me up
upon thigh   this is much

To envisage like the spin of the yellow street sweeper going at it now

And if there were another
beseech you to tell me

Had I not brought that lingerie into the dusk

Had we not
discussed it further

I would go for you to divine me

The forest sans darkness
sans wet muddy tracks

Spaces necessary to depart
in one finger's revolution

The skin has little breathing room

Previously it would have behooved me to illustrate the night was far the day long

You were legions off and nigh

re: shirts left out on the bed
re: la luna in an old postcard

You had gone/come back to this golden panel

No nethering its blackbirds
you were drinking coffee

Head bent over red counter shoulders smoothed

In sphere's harmony   you were so at hotel with me

Taking your hands from under the spigot   you were offering me a Lucky

Every. Youth. Was. There.

Love's Portfolio

A fragment
of a fair copy would undo our slant meeting,

an in-flight movie
where we chatted

how life was choosing not choosing.

Joy and gravitation,
the day turned

canonical,
                my book's cover and spine.

The sky blued
vagrant scribblings into print culture,

what shall be clad,
           the day's whole cloth.

A scribal hand,
a something.

A kiss away,   a kiss away,   a reader's
curve,

                  a reader's little addict
in black pants who would like to

        sit in the dust as Heav'n's other spangles do.

I lowered
I wrote the answers on whose hand
I approached
as an alias, trachea

                without sound,   my signature,   bright felon.

Beauty and the Beast

That the transactions would end.

That the rose would open
          (her appearance in a Cyrillic blouse),

leaving the sense
that one had reached for it—

dust gray blue green manifold red and torn,
          his studied performance of a romantic mood.

He is still eating other small beasts.

She is sleeping alone
coiffed in the pleated moments,

only rising to bathe before the mirror
with its grand so what.

But we who have held the book with both hands
and let the syntax shape us

we are not evermore
as mirror or sleep.

In our modern cloven space
events dissolve to the sexual instant,

each of us holding the hairy hand
with thrilling lucidity.

So we never find out what we mean
but it flakes off on our hands,

so the pleasures we most desire
go unexpressed,

people of the future will also have

light, fragile conversation
and a hidden cottage with shutters carved,

where each summer we return
with no misgivings, no spectacle—

Nothing to be afraid of.

Only the 18th century air,
making it impossible to breathe more purely.

And she is femaling him.
And he is maling her.

And someone says, the end.
And someone says,

no, this is my body.

Fuck the Millenium

A photograph a beautiful woman

A photograph of a beautiful woman

Now that's it, hold it   right there,
would you just turn the head a little to the side

White cypresses, telephones dangling out of

my sorry images

Certain unsteady figure in raincoat watching
          her counter figure
cross the street carrying on completely normal life

so she's feeling constructed but still has to walk around

Unseen historical figures
belligerent with obscene greed

reacting metaphorical to what,

who is dominant?

Rot me, rot me, cry the birds
from the flowering compost

particle drawn to particle, o optical day

Certain figure in raincoat
crying now

everyone passing by trying to look away

Culture
invading a huge hole in the realism

Not to achieve a mere semblance

Marina Tsvetaeva

left hanging too long
as no one wanted to be seen

as connected to that

Standing alone as through the sun

tragedy is glory in an ideal mirror

Standing alone as through the sun cut in strips
no ones sees us though we're watching

A beautiful woman photographing
a stand-off at the day-care center

A foiled bank robbery   made someone   shooting mad

Lipsticked on a banner: I don't want witness   I want cure

I held a good bird dying in my hand, archer

Let it be remembered I was linked with the use of the camera

Flute Girl

I kept coming in whenever anyone else entered,
like the drunk man,

or behind
Socrates, a sudden opening

like quick grabbing an extra newspaper off
someone else's coin

      before the latch shuts,
or the soft hush of the ATM card as it enters—

these are sounds
you may know intimately.

Love a silver reed.
Between the teeth.

      Some words
creaked
coming out of the rhetoric—

I was sent away.
Back into the opening.
        The blur of the other side
where I'm hidden
    though not exactly

stricken,
        beautiful and silent so that I may be lacking—

This is
what made me

audible to you.

Socrates

Predictably Socrates is late to the seminar on Socrates.

He is too at hotel with himself,

a place in his voice no sound comes through,

opposite of evangelist.

Like a situation in his dreams in which he couldn't.

All this could happen,

even to Mr. For Whom the Birds Must Stop Singing.

For us, too, so a feeling is changing, and soon   it's cut here,

what dawn is this

        humans tumbling

and the star hanging

enchant   as neon interrupts to rose.

No one can know what is wanted.

Before it all starts flowing into a different emotion.

The World

Sweet nullity.

You had come back to this red counter   with your thorny

everyman's hands   you were drinking coffee

behind plate glass,   a person experiencing a person's dimensions, a thousand-fold,

la luna in an old postcard.

Lesions etc., moon's tissue, etc.

Do not fix it in the eye—go !

Do not read it in the book—live!

Unrepeatable

as sky's folio:

The waitress's hands under the spigot   you were offering me a Lucky

Date Movie

How I had come to you,

how you had come to me,

the wind parting hair on the boulevard.
The night vendors,

the newspaper's blot,

the rain stopping into
the rape sheet and body tally

not the clean slate we crave,
our late bodies

worked into a fitness that keeps us like lambs fenced in a village,

in a "ruin of a culture," in a black rain—

The earth tilting
in apogee, or just like

      jackpot winnings,

we pray a good crosswind
gets us out of this barn place, that has no art.

So tell me how is it

Mary gets changed into a little girl in the arms of her son who henceforth becomes her father—

and does this make her still
his mother, his daughter,

or his wife?

Thus a wanderlust began

preceding the specificity of us,

(as in anticipation of
as in the theatre now

                      the velvet curtains parting),

and we turned our faces to the larger faces, and grew
to resemble such conditions
in the night damp

until there was nothing left to look at—

Between watching
and being watched,

were we a welcomed sight,

like when money
was first pinned to the madonna, the first parade?

Between
seeing and believing,

I love the liquefaction of your voice.

A treble in the high wire shiver if
I get a recorded voice,

how if we let the lawn go natural,

the insects will return,
faint discordant American rhythms

in the offing.
Come in, please.

These plums are still warm from the sun and slightly pungent in the crab grass.

Over our nakedness,
a thrown blanket's disquieting

undertow of air.
A live color broadcast over the moon, red drape.

The World

Some are born
some are born

               selfhood marches

                   across the surface an owl lifts on bony wings

Whose brain
Whose brain

          furnaced

the eyelash   the sparrow   the cat   the marguerite
the Floridas, the Mediterraneans,

o lawful bread
o wondrous portal

Here come our enlarged and nefarious senses

(a couple arguing old world
malarkey   under the honeyed streaks on-site

prestidigitous   platelets of cloud   floating past)

Here's a form
we need to fill in

        and hold lanterns and double space into

the password for
        how we found
        time to do it

time grainy and full   time mowing down

Some are born
some are born

silence throwing itself   asunder   spectre   joyous

Some are born

        who find use

        use some of this

        use this

IV.
FATHERLESS AFTERNOON

Profane Halo

This was the vernal   the unworldly human

        the most elegant car in the train.

A faithful and anonymous band of huntsmen,

a runner of red carpet

spotted with pheasants

on which an origin, a cold sun shone.

These were the black shoes,

the skirt one smoothed to speak.

The unknown tongue for which I am not the master,

chiefly the messengers

circling back through the vectors as the ashes adjust,

a loner with a hat,

a loner on a cold dark street,

a man gone away for cigarettes

on an otherwise calm evening.

And the signs that said yield, and then *Sssshh*, and then

let me sweep the porch for you.

A woman's black beads scattering into order.

Girl running along outside of herself toward.

Pale hopalong.

And time scarred up to do a beauty.

Dear Sunset that was sun of now,

Near Greatness, dear tongue my Queen, dear rock solid,

how could we know that we are forerunners?

The first characters in a crowd

and yet we were outwardly quiet.

We assemble here toward the river

or wherever the horse leads us,

dear oarsman   the valleys are green,

some bodies piled

some bodies marked and burned away.

New ones just wiped of their meconium.

In the whites of the lovers   in the evenings under.

Dear human mood   dear mated world.

There, there, now.

Dear ease of vicarious place, oil in sea.

Dear ravishment of fountain

figure in the fold.

These are the beers we drink like oxygen

in hats grown large as I.

The loner going door-to-door, the paint excelling

the door in cubes of prescience, durations of grey.

Here we attach the theatre of a girl

the miniature size comprehensible

the door a seed

the tree a dwarf

the hay a stack

the uncreated still.

Cool of the evening,

thine ears consider well

the uncreated still.

Huntsman in the quietened alley

in the dark-arched door.

Train long and harpiethroated.

Earth's occasional moonlessness

laying hands

on the data in the street,

under which   loose animal

the unbending pale of whose complaint   becomes the dust's surround

The River Replaces

The river replaces, the willow drags

a horseless rider caparisoned in red

glides over the gravestones.

Velvet is the integument I'd hope for for night.

Our doors are unlonelied

in the most diaristic indulgence, Death comes unexpectedly

and so you sure better

knock, and in a magnitude of scales.

The most full-flooded four-color process awaits there when I have time "for myself"

and cannot render it.

I had to guess "this was happening" said one self to the other

who self same said as the original broke

through the dream hole of the second,

and hurled its relapse into a momentary

acquaintance who ground significance with a tired pestle

until my sleepy lover woke. I had to shade the place

just so. Heaven it's heaven said it's heaven

pure heaven the self hands heaven's print-out

across a warm booth to another:

Heaven: Example

The heaven is without description.

Put them in one and the old will rage in a canoe.

Heaven was splashes of color

tossed casually from ecstasy to mania

so seeing had to become habitual,

seeing was certain films we could not look at,

films of commingstance. Might as well

bury me 'neath the blurry white oleander

crowding the pear tree near the family house

in its unassailable wedlock: personlock: what alchemy of emotions

to accompany speech

and bit o' pain.

A grave is goodbye last ditch so long see you again, adieu.

Always within earshot, actuality becomes you.

We needed the rain.

Indoors I worked like the crow, the phone rang.

I worked at it,

and the whole time I could hear you,

you didn't have to scream.

Here is a dark suit and tie.

Appearance illumines.

Appearance forgets it like an egotist.

Fathom thee.

Tincture of Pine

I am Citizen of the wind,   I am bird-infested

Data and regret,   the clouds purl two

unhitch
                    [why only one head, why only

two faces]

one for noontide   one for old horse in the mire

Furious are giants arguing over maps

History lays a violence under the peacefulness,
someone goes
driving the car

Let us go

through the porchlight

to the portal: No one and her white mare,   earphones of noise

No one lends her small ear

Poetry   before its raiment   coffin

a quiet word   the day   catching on

oh Marsha, why do you paint   the slop jar

Sunday Morning

Theriomorphic clouds color of sweet milk cast shade in darkest suit.

Idolatry, a man whacking at weeds

then a young girl lips to the dusty screen door

longing for the neighbor child,

leaves falling into sequence but not category.

Accidental openings of no rest, suffering she walketh along

the burning edges of the garbage bill as if into the day. Satellite

was one of those highlighted words on the spelling sheet because it contained

a double consonant, satellite to guide me, satellite to inform, to frown up at in outer
    space.

Seconds, minutes tocked as these, fast bug across the floor

will survive into that opening, and soul bargain

the body on its offer, eager in its youth. And extraordinary,

extraordinary was hard, smears of orange along the noun following,

blue violet haze of dusk beneath the screen door, ETC.

Who made the afternoon was a true hell-maker.

Dead, do you camp here under random oak,

a tree to pin down the entropy, leaves' drape?

Is there no covetousness enough, a flow to humanity and other such fleshpots,

accessible phones in the towers we heard ourselves reply to,

to make a winter arbor an espaliered

galaxy— the whole fabular whole

to unremain, the lawn green

and bilious, a misty absinthian sea

heaving at his feet as God queries from behind

the dry tree and into

a blue truck rumbling neutral then lurching forward

as we take that dark drive together,

in our great gravel of a thirst, God taking his first swig,

You lied about it, the hollow ambrosia, colors of horses, the double fictions of my mouth—

Native

Let me see
if I can understand you as part of the architecture

though it is the architecture of the place

that keeps killing me, dream of sky that stays
perfect blue foam, dream unfurling

gone and fusing like a hand that has fallen
into place.

You are at the pond

and the beach and over the want ads

and then I have the quieter
impulse to paint
beneath envy's carriage
along eternity's mill.

Earth kicking me up in the form of the human,

and taking the meaning
and giving back the meaning

as the photographs do with the life.

Before rheumy eyes
before young strapping eyes.

A mystery you didn't step over
the white painted hot dog stand

dwarf autumn marigold

a gold chain to look, and look away.

To looky here lies your
empty leg, your empty leg of even gin I would give you

for just the hint of I
I essence
I nuance up the flue.

For the rheumy eyes
For the young strapping eyes.

And begin bicycling a side road in the gaping jaws of

sweet anthem that plays
but follows like murder like entropy like lassitude,

a shade, and then a plain, and then a majesty.

Abandoned on the shore

                a red towel,

           oh my automaton odalisque.

The sun and the wind and the resultant white cloud

then the car gone off in yellow traffic like a "so there"

might we have in conversation,

as in who am I   to write this, who

Who   who is speaking   most whoever-ly,

Who, you are pale

though always

you are social.

As ever,   it is water from a spring

to walk with you

New

I says oh Jesus, can't I count on you people?

A zone goes   where sky's gone
what fresh hell for

burning and dodging, earth

more placid
where the state need not borrow. Have you seen the flowers on the river?

There is more to press them to, more

to compare. One has to swim through to find

this one   who had little to speak of.

This one who lay down though a motorcade went by.

Language of the west, please do run out into the ocean.

The art set crushed the tastemakers shamed Authority's myth layed out under a giant
    work light—

grid beware

the pile driving,

pile driving its two notes unevenly.

Some breeze   light rock in the kitchen   the dead crying not to be alive.

Human and elegant great structures Time glued,

one is seeing through slats as one

is ferried down Lethe, to green and neutral green, white trees, the dead Why

at the beginning of the question.   One

doesn't come home one wakens

Persephone to ask, have you seen

the daughters of Memory? Paper

is ash, eternity takes tumbling bodies into its apartness

One is turning away

Zero has a glade

One is a fiction

One is slow in the death

One dies out over you,

arm back in curved light

One is arcing back

One is not a fiction

Zero has a glade

The Pox

Paleopathologists   discover   invisible balm on   3,000-year-old mummies,

like trochees   in the terrorists' letters.   And in   the Americas, covering the sores,

9 out of 10   Narraganset Indians, "They die   like rotten sheep," wrote one colonist,

when armies flee   at sunset   and deliberately fan   the flames of,   deliberately fan

this lack of I   so heaven   so no one   I know   will die.   I with skin intact

as on a cream-colored page   or a slicked pond.   When I am dead   and

go unsaid,   stop worry,   don't look   for a raft of trouble.   A sister steps back

into her vector.   Word comes and we eat   at the fugue of it,   on the morning porch

the sun's   public bath of social space—   what if the poems preserve us?

So no one I know will die,   that's my   sister in

the sundown flame, in the feeling of

intimacy that is mineral,   bitter asteroid,

"for I have the warmth
of the sun
within me at night."

Lincolnesque

Peace does not appear so distant as it did.
Nor legs so long

as if to ask,
is this a marriage or an allegory?

Enter do you want
        a Negro woman for a slave
        or a wife?

"I could just leave her alone."

War next   next/next
over in less than a week, sure thing most excellent
chief, high hat with no man in, death close-walking—

Enter Captain Lilac
brought the enemy
down
but
enemy
resurrected
through
dooryard
last—

                a laughingstock, the green states,
who once had his
"persuasion, kind, unassuming persuasion."

* * *

One spiritualist, two spiritualists, three spiritualists,

four

dust off   black topcoat of history,
lilacs, lilacs, you and me,
we always got the histamine.

Sparrows nest
near the eyes, flee bearded Death,
concrete example:
"I am not reading. I am studying law."

Enter
        "a specious and fantastic
          arrangement of words,
          by which a man can prove
          a horse chestnut to be
          a chestnut horse."

                        * * *

Money to make rich sound
in school children's pockets,

money to know all their addresses, ordinary terrors
to keep under one's hat, muy tired.

Does poetry matter?

A cloud clearly seen is stranger than country, mystic chords and patriot graves, 'copter guard.

If Colossus could have sat down, I bet he would.

Free verse is "Ladies and Gentlemen: I appear before you merely for the purpose of
            greeting you, saying a few words and bidding you farewell.

            I have no speech
            to make, and no sufficient time to make one if I had; nor have I the strength

            to repeat a speech, at all the places at which I stop. I have come to see you
            and allow you to see me (Applause)

Enter the lawn from the rear,   grey/green, windless, eerie.
Unsifted birds layered low

lift to the oracle's ear, whippoorwill intoning over rio. (Great head above crowd,
brow in the cirrus, that's you,

spoken man)
Imagination to state:

concrete
over the dead, piled-high.
Shadow returns the sight
to wonder.

            and now I believe I have really made my speech and am
            ready to bid you farewell when the cars move on."

This Land Is My Land

Her bosslady trousseau was crepuscular.

Her remarks half-uttered

the documentary sound of the day.

Traffic salted   the nothing happening parts,

the whole had been

the whoever-you-are,

frozen, or instamatic,

the rise/fall   orbit,   some kind of

guide figure at the window,

a silence tangled there.

A rim painting over the sun

in which

history would like to do a little unwriting, futurally.

History writing,

spare me.
I am afraid I will die like this,
a human face, of late.

No one understands
the writing.

The words keep saying

        is that

our wordy bride?   Cancel and begin

      oh no,

         she is a dark contemplative.

The Victorian was once a farmhouse.

She was in the task of her biography.

Attention's fan.

In a gorgeous relativity

a bit like reading the markers

in a botanical garden,

California floats its prisons in the sea.

A Little More Red Sun on the Human

A little more red sun on the human   Church program spiked to the tree

There where the child carved   Grown to the father

Daughter in the grassy lot   sky pink-streaked in raincord   Forgive

my fallen corporeality   Once I was the first germ of life

afloat in the swampy gale   Water drop, come roll away the stone,   a polaroid I pan

The world is terrifying   The land covers up

The land says to itself its eternal doubt   Green trees

are bending, tombstones

are bursting,   a boy laughs   in lag time

Aphoristic   ferryman   The community's

leafy vernacular   meaning all life

is unfinished   as the grass

grows back   The mourners bow   every so often   over the human

The river's candor   a life sentence

Hazy,   launched, stopped

Vision this honeyed outline

The shapes   suggest

it is late   afternoon   Did you   know it too

Fatherless Afternoon

Fatherless afternoon, very untitled death,

partial the anatomically endowed
tree burl that gathered many before it

along the hike the country road glorifies the human gait

the human gait developed over berries
harsh and crude

then perfected in the lunar shafts I sleep for—
I was in the life class

wanting to copy copy copy it as becries the scrivenor,

the inability
of white birch
grazing the picket fence,

yellow smearing blue across the palette, white spackled

into sky over river
over upside down chair bobbing up
from the river

it is all waking up only to feel like a freak.

Do not simplify
any whole paradisiacal tale,

river held and rolled
against the small divisions,

most minute cloud displacements
please extend sunfallen hours.

Thousand words,
don't eat this.

*   *   *

Gray suit in the shape of the drapes there   busy one with texture

figure through flowered walls with open unexpressed lips

you are the big picture, my eyes to foliate later.

Window at rest now dusty in its corners, no one calling

as the lowering pink clouds
surround the motel

     ecstasy

ecstatic the sparrows
in bursts in trees
above the Western American fence.

And fatherless afternoon I spend you,

big gold watch and chain
big gold watch and chain

Dingy pool of sunlight

the white mule drinking there

Lucky stag in a waterfall

lucky stag

washing perfume from your moonlit shirts
Tide brings the one who loves you

Tide pulling the world

but you must not attach

*   *   *

God please drive slow

Contain no voice   presentable
contain

no sun   bleaching the roof,

throning   deepshaded   eden

No failure to love

longevity of

no   failure to love

the strain in every bird

fantails   scattering wind and dirt

small blue worm   on the half-eaten map

must not attach

Turning the mobile, handling
the long black snake,

thorn and crown

sky weirds
the empty lot

there is work to be done

drive slow

grave bride
with a black boutonniere, shorebird on the roof

do you feel a little displaced   so high
over the underwater lawn.

*   *   *

Orchids
snag on one's bodice, pearls abide,

still water

stewing   tangled vine, country gate   do not attach.

The guide figures
go psalming,   patching

the chants,
secrets of mine flesh is heir to.

Census returns
of California

census returns of California
fail to indicate

the ocean has a sunlit zone, a twilight zone, a deep ocean, and abyss.

It is a world of complete darkness, bitter cold, and crushing pressure.

Extraordinary

creatures who live here,
            do we say after this is all over,

you climb the stairs of a big white farmhouse
where love inclines?

Wild roses on the fence existing,

robust with something in the human makeup,

land of shades, trembling

of sea

Painterly, Epigean, Dream's Hangover

A griever in a party hat
    come to lay like a corpse
    before the weeper.

Stifle me not with the opposite.

Witness the gaiety of red socks,
    I have always been
    comic to you.

Let me entertain the yellow leaves
from white birch,

let me

before I die before I die

walk
as if for the first time
    upright into the depth perception

so that I begin to shade the place.

I am loving

variously

the far lateral
    of sidewalk
    the rough sequences

of getting somewhere.

Shall we go

home now,

a little preoccupied?

If you flirt with height
    with an appetite for distance
    you will get
    exposure:
    the brain senses the body
    is too far
    off the ground
    and shuts down
    such convexities.

As interstate widens
vowels shorten

    the farther north you go.

Leaves dip into an altogether
    other climate

the houses hurt the activity maligns the letters fade over the pilot light.

As before but with the senses disarrayed at what one can say.

It's bewildering but I can get you out of storage.

On the last five evenings of a life the newspaper still read

is this necessary?
We are way beyond the elucidative stage.

To set forth thy other foot, to know of one's errand.

Oranged
sunset,

the melodies run counter.

Not known   not done

a form occurs
                              occurs
creation

attaches more world

Birdman

I feel this tragic figure sitting on me

as stars dot to dot over the water that is potable.

As shoeblack in the hair will defoliate the scalp.

As lyric, lyric cries the verb, speaking of the thing.

(As the lawyer looks around for an ashtray.)

The ferry's arc   the ferry's lamp

the inchoate sumac   the inchoate sumac's blonde wig

tossed casually now above the rocks.

City as the merciful end of perspective,

city as.

He said   may we talk briefly so that God can be glimpsed

and alongside human conversation.

Heron.   Hilarity.   Time,

hilarious white spoonbill that cannot be held in the mind.

Erotic ripple marks on shore

failing to prove one's presence,

my halting attempt in the gusting spray.

Yes, sir.   Yellow pine.

Some are more released by words. For some hell *is* other people.

He wears a green eyeshade cap, like an aging umpire,

in January 1943 issue of *American Canary*.

Title: "I Wonder."

He spoke for the pillars, the bars, the sea air, the perpendicular pronoun,

the little gods running around the rocks with small black cameras.

Sometimes I too feel like a motherless

says the lawyer,

neural damage, agrees

the doctor, each to each and in their horrible penmanship.

And nature does not abhor.

Once I was a House Sparrow

now I am a Yellow Hammer

One

One
privately
owned airplane
disappearing into
business
you could fancy it
the most melancholy sound in nature

a place to sprint from the center

new
in scale the screen

making memory the eye following

the screen   more Chaplinesque
                than ever

the picture pouring soot on you/   Your morning coffee of ash

shoes on the detached stair
more-than-time   breaking the heavenly scape

What
should we tell the citizen?

"I think
all my guys
are dead"

The citizen softly projected toward the building

That was something did you

                              see that?

Who
picks up
a shovel

When there is nothing to contain
                    you

minister to
doctor to

Night wounds, let me introduce you
to the day wounds

flag off a yacht

over a plank in reason
flaps back

flapping back

The Garden

The world news wants more than a little exile, is it that you were trying
to lie down too much in red dirt with dusk?

Sirens mean the garden is partially thumbed out.

And I have a smudge on my cheek, the bird is being incoherent with me.

The last rite, the third
witness, more news lurking over the waiting dinner.

Repositional clouds reveal less and less a blank dossier.

No rest for you, My Wicked.

My Elected Officials are Falling into Historical Moments

In the stray world I drive my tractorlike car
through the capital
fain I would read the wall

in the roadside toilets light anoints a sky
prayers in my gullet like a wounded soldier
stone asleep on a cold floor

at the postal station I awake and out of the p.o. boxes pop all these penises
each with a pink ribbon

just like yesterday, says a voice I am descended from
gathering watercress beside the river to make these delicate sandwiches
at streetcorners' deserted babel manifesto and other sounds of death

Three Figures at the Gates of the Gully

an airport by matchlight

no usual   links   thick the clouds

in the form

of unsayability—

for a change,

it's poetry that neglects the capital

Burnt City

Nitrous,   blanched,   another   hole in space   a tiny armpit   a flower

a spot of blood   on the blank document,

the tyrant and the harpy   circling the foundation,

chasing one another,   the night a color killer   the vector

twirled and shut

in the hydraulics in which night flings forward

to touch your finger

to liberty,

to feel bruised by redemption,

the plasma that constitutes,

a way to say

people ARE worth the effort

though they heat and crowd one another

in the wrong quadrant of the brain,

if we demur

breasts of a kind person

a starlike illogic

* * *

One stopped chugging engine
the lyric fashioning a flute

of rivercane,

Andy shot so the mylar balloons.

The multiples and multiples of Marilyn
                    ancient sources tell us

                    pale and ruddy
                    olden days, a city

                    one little flap of secret longing,

                    and eventual

                    pockets of smart management,

                    hot plates,   and on the third day,

                    crème brulee   international

policy to animate, to gladden

Dug out in the ground in November

                                        the undermall listening through its holes

                        *   *   *

Like giants with all our might

unmediated in one's dark apartment,

tower   from which the hair defoliates,

an I
of yore
                        as the sun

supinates, transfixes there,   red twilight

                                    like giants with all our might

high-hatted ones on pintos under sun

an imaginary   liberty

                        *   *   *

Our eyes,   cameras

delicately strapped to our heads
we could barely feel them,
a grey transfer

tucked into the goal,

but that part was filmed separately, and in another laboratory,

a heady wine in golden palaces

my missing one, last breath into cell phone sweet everlasting one

be still, a makeshift

a national infancy

makeshift
another national infancy

nailing something in,

* * *

hunger be luck and gangplank.

A harpy chased a dog on her embroidered pillow.

And then she blew smoke into the robocop's bosom.

World silence picture shows,

red sun under eyelids,

we have just about

had it

with reality's blazing gunplay.

Skull be dogbone, syllabary hung

like wash, sun mortal beautiful because it can destroy

historical time,

        the wind, the wind martyr

                      *   *   *

no giantism to take the trees

a single red ribbon in a day book   a folded fan

a day a tide a day   a whipswitch that comes one way

a spoorless quietude   hell does not wish to   sip anymore   "Integrities"

                                            can make

                                            somebody poor

Unsullied white flowers

of form and the form of darksome cloud

pine lanes and the fresh horses who fly into them,

fly through them,   fly in

Every Epoch

dreams it has been destroyed by catastrophe.

                      a mass ego only properly exists in earthquakes
and catastrophes,
                      a mass ego as in music,

the one song everyone loves.
but the violence one has to incorporate is great,

                      the joy is mighty,

                      the one song everyone loves, loved.

every epoch dreams time is a water garden in a weedy churchyard.

no Hell in your draft

there are other terrors.

                      I sleep
                      You sleep
                      He she it sleeps
                      You sleep they sleep we sleep.

the incomparable moon chapter, over mine enemy.

                      strong leader dozes off in horizon's dank corridor

                      calm nights along sensorium's riverbank.

objects freed of their utility completely unmoored.

an epoch dreams and one follows any adversary on land,

any adversary

in the bottom of the brain,

an enemy sitting across from a lover,

calmly editing a lover,

her salad a mirage.

a real world could come back to us as an epoch,

similar to a short while and a further example.

ecstatic child leaning over a pickle barrel.

a time bruise on the pickle barrel.

a few masterpieces droop, an epoch

dreams in the ruinous thereof.

every epoch dreams, and one follows.

every epoch dreams, one follows

as a figment in one setting beyond this earth even.

It Was the Beginning of Joy and the End of Pain

The sewing machine had a sort of genius, high, oily and red

over that little hellion's pants.   Joy and Pain crossing legs,

then coloring in the poverty—

Are we a blue, blue whine in the restive trees?

Are we under the imprecision?

The beginning endless, ending like chasing deer out of the yard,

sphere unto sphere it takes a loyal Enthusiast
to be
Death's mother. Stag on the meadow,

mare in the river,
unwinding green river   wide rock for the resting.

The man and the woman liked to go there,
sprawled across

the warm hood of the car, a question under sky, a curve where the trees rustled.

A patch of brown hair on the white clapboard
where the deer tried to run off
scraping its side,

harsh light in the paint can,
                              weightless

the screen door until you
heard it click shut.

She placed the shell and the action figure beside one another.
Who is king, my queen, as many tongues as there are swords.

Gone to field, weeds sway, some places are still
semi-barbarous you can make a fire under the bridge and smoke.

A headless man knows
how you saw what the saw sawed,

and there is usually enough poetry
to pass out,   the day is ongoing,

you can get more material there
a rough sleeping   writ large.

I loved playing that hand harp,   large face
coming to ask   Who are you,   Where   is your precipice?

The pattern crying, the pins too many colors, surround, surround.

The pattern crying you be the master, I'll be the life,

have I been in this T-shirt all day, did I sleep in it, first did I see it this morning.

Was that you bound in sun on the step, living the life of the seasons, and loving,

I am recalling nothing of the unloving of ourselves,

did you not foreshorten into pattern one thing from its happening,

where you arc slowly dying in a city,

I am born in a town.

Middling in a hive

nothing is daring to move anymore.

Sticking our feet into a template of lakes,

it is endless, endless and endless a schizy feeling walking back into your world

V.
MORE LIVES

Culte du moi

We are captains of fatigue. The sound is an enterprise. Serial balconies along the street.
I miss the sound of typing one letter at a time, and many machines typing letters at
the time. When I was loping through the yard one day, I felt like Whitman, it was
the closest I got to feeling like a man though sometimes in pickup trucks, there was
Paul Bunyan. Once under the dappling elms I became two innocent boys who kicked
a basketball onto the lawn of the scary man's scary house, and when the scary man
came out to chase the boys away whose basketball it was he died of a heart attack he
was so angry and unable to speak the basketball, the word basketball, as when you
open your mouth and nothing comes. We are captains. So far over 6,000 of us have
died, depending on who you talk to. Our bodies are imitations of the spirit and our
statues are imitations of imitations, per Plato. Our bodies hang from rafters, magnolias,
lampposts and telephone poles. When all has been said, and has been argued to no end,
it begins to rain on the pictograph. Our buses reek worse than the people on them, our
buses carry us anywhere they are extraordinarily accepting urine reeks but rarely stains
when you get down to it you smell it much more often than you see it, unless you look
back, and I try to take off my steaming boots. I can't give away my sleeping dogs. A
pinafore a piano forte a fugue, I got the best job in the world by just being myself and
then I fell forward arms lifted into a pause of music arrested in the idea with my eyes
closed I am usually happy to do anything for art, but this was a job not a wandering
aim. I got it and then I quit so as not to ruin. I tried to tell everyone everything I
thought they wanted to hear then I became a captain a fatigue. Once a plagiarist tried
to steal me but I ran and ran faster into a tumbling, refreshing stream, then I stood
in a long line waiting for bread. Her Lawrence brought his face home still burning to
death from the war. No one comes to thank the steam for the engine, no one regards
the cow when you can get the milk in fraying grids of lace. I plan the day in finding
in Poe a soul-brother by whose insight I might maintain a growing boy of uncommon
experiences and opportunities. I usually see a house in the distance.

Schools of Thought

The world is a weird luminescence.
A greenish glow, unhinged.
It is unruled by a dowager, an empress, a Madonna, a lopped-off head, a great red disc.

We lay sleeping in the arborvitae
and cypresses and ferns,
unsurprised and semi-conscious, not knowing
which is more fictional—the hand in the book,
or the book in the hand.

All-powerful nudes stepping into showers
our bodies a series of planes
best rendered in oils—
we are not untouched
by Modernism, though to stay modern is too much work.

Most ideas have their secret motives.
The earth has its arenas
cross-cutting on top, under, inside, combusting far away into a space probe.

The future is a probe, tied to its fear
of stopped time, or the half memory
of a kind of cyber hell
in which we fled the hedged passage.
Sunspun the bureau for the fleece of gold.
Or all is forever
created and creaturely—

a multiverse
without a manual

in which someone who is not you,
but an exact replica of you, is holding a book

in a room or a public space or a mode of transport that is not where you are,
but is an exact replica of where you are,

on an earth which is not the earth
but an exact replica of the earth
on which you stand
as if on an uninhabited plain,
and it is not a distancing to compare
not a photo not an image
and there doesn't seem to be direction though there is wind,

there is no time but the light remains.

No one is weaving a great shroud
and no one is unweaving a great shroud
but the weave is present because it is
thought about and the weave is taut.

If you look, I have turned
to face your shore, and have come from far away
composing a path of words or word thread

in which perhaps we share a hope for others
even if they are half dead, and lying between us,

we recognize them in their shredded clothes
in the tin types or live feeds and reach out
to wipe their brows, not there, thin air—

Sunlight piercing oxygen
clean through we are imagining again that we are no one and
every variety of nuisance of no one

and so we are kind of
allied

and following a conversation
made as we are of molecules and lament
where an intelligence lives.

And whether I am on the replica of that intelligence,
or on the intelligence itself,
it is no matter,

we stand as if on an uninhabited plain,
and it is not a distancing to compare

not a photo, not an image
and there doesn't seem to be direction, though there is wind,

there is no time, but the light remains,
and you do not look back.

Romance

inharmonious red stars   satellites not even stars   over a line of taxis

(extend your hand, extend your hand, bring me high words and locusts without end
dormant ((someone has to take over))

like the two drinking the last of their alcohol in the apartment

two sleeping it off later

one rolling over calm as a ballast— slow glissando of a muscle group caught under sheets

porch swing in— wind in didn't we need
the rain— the swing in—   rain

forcing the earth to smell the earth, the dung of the two

sleeping in

in what anyone will do next, springing tiger

My Name is the Girl with One Glass Eye Said Bitterly

My name is the girl with one glass eye said bitterly.

                                        Nightingale

in the birdfeeder hung from the pepper tree opening throat to the body

of light in (was it spring?)

                        spring's shipwreck—

high voices. lank hounds

ramping it up over a highway arcing out into empty air—

where we

were resiliencies at the edges of time

dining on upended peach crates—

on lawn chairs dropped into the shaded pool

of the bottomless—where through the murk

Muses and Mediums regenerate the pool's Eylsian scum. I am the girl who opens the seashell

that stirs the cauldron

that sings us back to the leafy path witch-worn and cobbled thru—

What do you walk upon?

Something already

in the blood.

What line of work you in?

job is Job is Job is job is Job it's all part of an infinite

series foci aperture
2/3 ¾ 1/8 scherzo   pattern I get it,

you look like someone I used to know

drinking out of a garden hose.

Can we summon by the hooks in the water

all the broken—as in the belly of an unsuspecting

mother—can we open the open

the hatchback to hear the Gothic echoes—a virgin forest asway amid the Giant's sperm?

Tomb for Tit,

come, wounds—extension cords carried to a midnight execution and left

to dangle there, a beheadedness played over

and over culture soaking it up   I knew a Garden:

meaning of the world is intaglio of   it's sunny and 75.

What do you walk upon? Something already in the blood drafts an ink,

reconstitutes the flowers. Do you feel a light in the sun

on your back, piercing through the water, it's a light—said the said the I

am the girl with one

glass eye said

bitterly, now let me go, she said, holding the flowers to

long opal tails of moon waving slowly

from time to time

saying No no no no no no no, I am

the girl now that we are on the page of infinite

length,

in the city of uplanded height, on the lawn of rising

green   in the alley tunneled

down to a chambered core,

and I said how many people did you see on the road rolling up their old kit bag

how many people did you see

trying to get where trying to get there

trying to see the many people you have seen on the road

under the star's starkness under the exits entranced

under the mistral of

rain

feeding the lengthening stream we step into—out of—shuttering—

   pictured there

Brad And Angelina

To have to not have the actors get acquainted before (they shoot)

so awkwardness
of two characters feels like

awkwardness of two characters in marriage therapy

makes good disturbance in the field
genius on director's part both

hired assassins
unbeknownst to each other

assigned to kill each other
IS marriage

"I've missed you,
honey"

lit metropolis is writing
and could get to be event

if Brad and Angelina
would just get out of the way of tiny pinholes in the social mindscape

Angelina's critiqueless good thighs
making fine urban murals

"Papadaddy, you comin' to me now!"
Angelina occurring

Brad floating by no time even
high and dry it is best

to be the subject, not just about it,
a kind of prayer one utters silently

then enters like Angelina's faint vagina musk
Brad's sheep-a-leaping

Why do they walk the walk
and talk the talk that they are taller than we are
their heads brush the rain

The voice tells us Brad's seaside villa,
the faint vagina musk the penis smoothness enormity
of places, people, and things

To dare to put your own hands on your own hips
and stroke her shoe horn,
the breathless breasts and wild rock the Brad

that is the equal of the cliff head of cheat grass
the hinged panels of the human hand

Unpeopled climbs the steeple, a pulley-system,
Angelina's lips parting and coming together again in a scarlet lake

in the expanding of time
by the internal

proliferations of oriental
storytelling
a clown shaking his own hand and slapping his own butt

"Say,

,   ever been

in this part of the country
before?" inquires Brad,
huge smoke-drag trailing
out of his nostrils

as a bloody murderess hobbles out of her Ramcharger into the vet clinic
to loot supplies for her wounded leg
giant grasshopper
lighting on the white hood of the Ramcharger

gold sun
on the grasshopper's tough and pliant
breast plate

Would you rather

a. love an enemy
b. dream of dishonor of a loved one
c. exhibit fatal ambition by duty to country
d. talk crops or play jackknife

asks the half-clad native girl, resolutely placing her spear into the mud,
so that all night long a rain falls down and refreshes the field.

Frankenstein

I, too, would like to know why
I should like to speak to you again of the sea,

or at least hear again   in the time before,
first the social body was alive and warm.

Psyche giving birth to her child Bliss—
those were the days when I was in my ass form.

A dragon's purse,
exhausting work in my day.

                    Something and Nothing

arguing with my master, all because her descriptions were dying—

The other day Something was up and walking around
for an instant,
not realizing it was Nothing—

(how stupid can they be?)

Something and Nothing on the road

the blood flowing   the oxygen flowing
over dandelions and spiders

Something and Nothing
dead tired before their blocks of solitaire

the green banks
the icy hut upon the mountain

their wandering hands rowing my being

Readers still to come

Shorn Polecat, the Helping Verb for Which
One Must Keep One's Ear's Low

We had a taste for celebrity and had once bitten fame.

Along the lower serifs of the city,

a long red scarf to represent temptation.

Why do new poets want to gather round dead poets

and sing?

Oh, it's like chivalry, some would say,

the walnuts falling hard on the roof.

Human, a welcoming figure opening up the melon, making cole slaw
   of the important passages.

Wild parrots in the palms of their western city.

From the widow's peak, an outlawish look-see.

The effigy, in-law, dry leaf, fresh paint, dry rot smell of the old paperback.

In the real world there are no real maps, clippety clop.

A damp and moldy proof.

Living and dying we lay waste.

~~And~~ sit down ~~to it.~~
~~And~~ for a spell.

under shade of porch

a respite

Do We

do we really need words to stay within the sentence
especially when it is not a long tradition, either

it is an exquisitely
painful way to continue

to stand
in that cut,

changing our shape
utterly in the similarly deadly intimacy, staggering the imagination

western sea, western sea, a thought stream and a fantasy need, western sea, western sea

will you be my shapeless nonentity under the ancient olive tree

Tyger

Tyger, one paw curled under, the other splayed out

Sphinx-like

Jungles forget their laws systems their systems

Pronouns like to flee   he who she me

Be pieces in our hands

Making protoplasts and grasslands,

More lives, see how they square

Tyger having drunk of human hormones in spilled lake

Tyger rearing on hind legs a blurry fracas walking straight,

Tyger jumping across rooftops, the storylines played out

In shots of lights, silhouettes crosshatching

In dark windows, the fire-breathing lakes.

Tyger flying over couples in their birthday suits

And deathwear, sunbonnets, shrouds and towels,

Humans punching numbers with stubby fingers in scanned light,

Cashback, hello, wassup, a wail of train and forest parting, Tyger

In a smear of black and yellow stripes

Chasing above the naked, the goddamned and golden armed

Black revolvers out car windows

Tyger in the faint blue nightfalls

Streets scooped out in fearful

Liquefaction to the stripes, the better butter.

Hitchcock

Could we get by on a polytonic breeze, an aery charm?
A blonde sinking fathoms in the earth?
Could the convertible turn jade
along dreams and dream cliffs growing quiet and magnificent things,
such as night again, day again.
A silent forest ranger had been assigned him.

Bonds falling off
which hold one tethered to the ground,
we are free to dominate the valley like a master.
Slow curve of the earth
as if held by a small boy
on his way to school, the sun
perched on high,
not too far away.
Stairs lead up. A red scarf lands there.
A suitcase opens to a bus station.
Who wants to go back to that terrible time,
everyone smiling discretely, as though forgetting about the war?
Pale kimono in the closet in case we had got blasé
about death being loose in us.

So our lives are spiral staircases spiraling
avid and previous
with kills on either wayside.
Is this scary?
On the edge of the world a long line of black trees.
He wore a pink nosegay to his social skills class.
Winds gusting in the northwest.
We listen to one another breathe.

Sam Fuller

I am thinking of my future in a suitcase of champagne.

Door to door traveling black wash/white palette I have

big brushstroke I breathe underneath.

Staggering back from the slap I talk Big Daddy.

I'm still your sister under the hairy foliage.

Après retrieving French peasants from a Nazi cave,

the dogs they are sleeping and the children

are fed, heads bobbing in the backseat.

Human asleep in the sound booth,

crack of this pinecone, those rocks—

swish-swish of dark trousers of twilight—

white seagulls on the black jet

beach, your mother wasn't home

you walked to the sea

Cassavettes

Black hairdo moved in the frame for the question.

What's that inky noon what's that incarnation?

I don't need God to talk to, I need someone with skin on, says the man in the T-shirt,

invoice enumerated like a phone bill or the Bill of Rights

on the bedside table.

Out the window a midday glare of lampposts and fenders.

In black and white we are ruby-throated

on the white mattress of dishevelment, thinks the man in the T-shirt,

but he doesn't say it. Likewise,

you gotta seek love in a desperate city, says the woman

wordlessly in the black hairdo,

sending the whole heat of her love to the man in the T-shirt,

and this without shamefacedness.

When you get there, phone, says the man in the T-shirt, lighting a cigarette and waiting.

Jazz, not some deep-dust hillbilly record.

Completely un-mental pieces of time falling on them

in the water tap drip, two

on the edge of the bed drinking and smiling and laughing and walking

to the mirror at the start of the room, actions

beginning within them, actions about to begin.

Actions saying let's go,

as they adjust their clothes and comb their hair, carelessly

down the napes of their necks,

heads huge on the wall,

bent victims of love, undying shades to say the words from.

Tenderness of the Dove

Like a vulture to a graveyard.

Like a Brueghal to a red or a Guernica to a black or a Krasner to a hot orange.

Air vague, and best to know it than to not,

And revolution, at least half human soul my brethren scores of death.

Satan knew this about existence and its eves.

Thought is the flowing tap of error and perception,

A voting moron before a neutral ph

Paper, medium surface suitable for pencil, crayon or pastel.

Or what if before sunset we start to drink.

And oil breasts and groins and let loose all other genitalia.

River river river well river river river well

Kitten down the,   rope asway,

Post-crime hands in the sub-daylight   distended joy!

Why in the trees one bird should disabuse another

As one drives past them,

As one's neighbors yank palms from the earth

So the rat can no longer live there.

And one drives on

But yields no power, no ultimate authority,

But is only *apparent* as the birds close up the hole, as the birds cohere.

Paradise

It is hard to be at the right funeral.

Sometimes two columns form.

Some like to think of Beckett, some like to think of Williams, each

with a typewriter, returning.

The funicular and the nightingale

and the closed rooms we like to indulge them in.

A submissiveness.

A white heron, angular and hard, watching from the top of the tree, watching the water and the waste.

No vertigo along the tracks—as one car creaks up, the other goes down, faceless.

The heron taking off and landing, then awkwardly turning away, refusing to move.

No One Tells You Like It Is

NO ONE TELLS you like it is. I think it was warm that day. Sound and pulse the whales spouting such imaginary languages, chime and time and slap be lie we woke on deck not slaves, not surrogates, the atmosphere unfurled to what most could recall before the rains, the several gates. I think it was warm that day we did not stay inside dimensional limits of "natural selections," the marryings/buryings/buzzing cries—but sensed the prelingual in the nearly dead, and felt with each sun the limp limbs of the just woken nodding "yes" to the Yes—I think we were pedaling by a busted screen door somewhere in the house slamming back and forth in the scent of jasmine and dried plums—germination, maturation, rot—the river urging us, the returns of the four winds knocking aside the machines and all along the burning eye   the instant of meaning the hide seeks of Tyger

Sound of Freeways Directing the Cosmos Back to its Start

Death's got some spiraled plenitude in the distance between clocks,

both a velocity and a stasis at large. A fly curves its legs in

dioptrical, tense moments of rest on the window sill.

Try not to stare

at the white tiles in a urinal

and think what are you

doing here postcard face

postage stamp face

both believing and disbelieving

a harder time can come, which keeps believing around.

In the amniotic first few

       moments of the film arrive the windshields

we can move in,

       hot cold color smears of full-length

       characters drawn in master stroke

suck in the cul de sac's

    diurnal rotational breeze,

the certain blond dream of the sun going down

and the gates opening up. A modesty,

    the nice folks returning to nice homes, a little more tired,

no one dying miserably of too much Williams.

A willow, bay bark underneath, wet pulp

inside, twisting up to night sky.

Do you still have that project, I don't even have half a project, but if you had a project

we could blow them toward one another.

Let me entertain you.

We are here to entertain.

To hold the black whips

to embroider the day of the week so as to assign it

to the towel. If it's morning, what to read, cut off, wave, tie to the emergency cone?

Or if you are waking in the audience, what small clearings will you make

to rest from those of us in paradises and hells

also, the ecstacies of clover sprouting near manholes

amid the thrown down tissue through which we feel

we can see it all—   The hillock, a tall oak makes a shade above it,

and propped up against the trunk

reclines a leisured figure into which we can climb back in and read

toward the tonal promises

and geographical distances connecting inside our ears at the end, the dead

dark stallions the world lets go into meadows,

the man turning into a boy

walking through those archways

as we watch, holding his hat

on a dirt road, hearing ourselves implore a strutting mystic whose trading hand

is broke. Someone adds elements to the sentences the way a girl out west

just laughs. We had lyric time, we had pylons and pylons of it,

under low lying reefs of cloud the 8 notes

necessary for infinite melody, a convective heat event.

The faces swirling, the little hands uncurling, resuscitating to stay the world of awe.

The tiger sleeps until it is hungry, and then the tiger hunts.

VI.
DO YOU BELIEVE

an oh   a sky   a fabric   an undertow

an oh   a sky   a fabric   an undertow

a blanket laid upon the grass

all the mixed faces   looking out or looking in   the great paintings

in yard sales and museums   abstract or representational   oils   acrylics   ink

in the poem the evening is spread out

like a media

to let the windbag

out of

     to neutralize

our eternal Footman   who is presidentially nimble

and wears a big gold middle ring   to rap us on the head with

        when the sky   is a slow moving sea life

a poker tell, the solitary night finches   nested deep, dead asleep in urban bamboo's

tall corridors

          no longer a president

only an invisible indivisible male muse   all oscuro dark substance

molecularly swarming

in fields in cities   like a cloud rising from sidewalks

        to make individual appearances

so shaded so shrouded in oil

Whistler could have done him

sometimes appearing   in well-cut overcoat

or next to a tall case clock

to say look this was the deal

made a long time ago

can you give me a ride   to the vacated cities with most hospitable ports

A couple of lonely men had plans that got shoved this way

for a building we could aspire to enter

I donated   then got distracted   for a building we could enter

perhaps we shouldn't   (aspire I mean)

but it is good to build it now, as then

I am entering the poem now   not just to notice the pronoun I

but how casually the no longer   a president has used it

The sky   is a sea

we all committed before sinking into

the most hospitable port   where dust plays dark

before flying   invisibly into

undeadly messengers   done up as citizens

so it's all substance

to make   our children's lives   better than now

a situation I would take

as conduit, as altar   our groceries

there is a lot of room for metaphysics   in this country

I call waiting

the GPS navigational finding device   enhance search   the overly

Google mapped,   severe lack of frontier in the world

so lots of people have begun   exploring the sewers, recording

sounds of manhole covers as cars

roll over them   Only 12 feet down   it feels like 100

and there are rubber boots called   waders but they fill up

quickly   and are discarded   The idea is to tramp

what all gets transformed   back into earth's core

I would like to take some of that infant stardust that has fallen on your head

Why can't I be shrouded in it   if only undercurrent

I used to say my sister sold time on the radio   because that's what she did

but then television leveled

soundscape   the please of the palm tree rustle   in the gelatin print

internet   cresting event   manual or mental   a loose sally of the mind   all of it

suggesting streams   of attenuated speeches by absent friends   who said time

we're no more living   in a landscape   beyond end of the river valley

of that particular program   Now time says   it will save a working copy

of the image   with a slightly different name

My sister and I continue   to run up and down the stairs

Now I will give her a feminine ending

or an infant star fabric   to unfurl   The lonely men

were right to want to fold

their flags back into a triangle   when someone died

We could unfold   and try once more to open

a language in which we do not do

most of the killing

A drop-in date for the ungrievable   Some

will always refuse this country   to come forward

We could all take off our skulls and stare into them   A static in the

contours   rank waterfalls   gray green opal stones   the alert

pianist   key phrases of the Arcadians Indo-European root-rot doo-wop

The dead   re-circling   rocky crags where recline   the born   or birthing wet

with their last or first words   We could take   our fallen off temperate fur

and begin to recite a Greek story   a groan

now   see how fast   now can go

to what does it matter   world to come   word

to hold in the mouth and swallow

Untapped   what does it mean

if there is no way to say it if you haven't heard it before

so we are all writing writing writing and people say there are too many books though it seems to be reading that refuses to die   This is the good part

the part looking at the part

Can you tell if this is the good part,

you can tell if this is the good part

if it is the part looking back at you

not wanting to see someone else

airbrushed all over you

It is the feeling of being embodied by the person

you love, or are sweet on, enchanted by—

not that they fill you, but that you

are them, they've come to live inside you,

you look like them

you are so them   you see through them

and imagine they are looking at you,

being them, so

where are you

I am still beautiful

Experiments in Patience I

Vale of soul making—

            The cottontop tamarin
            & the common marmoset
            approach.

            The tamarin eats insects
            with quick jabbing strikes
            while the common marmoset

            must wait for days
            for gum to flow
            from trees.

Six signs you need to detox—   Patience broods and peacocks

Virtue stirs the pulp

I will wait for the God who hides   the hosannah   of what is received right in my eyes
to escape me

Unfiltered sun
an elevator down

                 a species

                .

                 of dandelions,   yellow splashes

The Patient

I am patient. That is my mineral fact.

    I have long term storage in double helixes

my two long polymers of nucleotides

    my backbone made of sugars and phosphate groups

joined by ester bonds.   I see imagist pears dissolving down

golden arms I hear needle-less the sleep aid cd's

    real violins, then float blue-black

at the eventide, injure

    of the taut to and fro, cut-back

asphalt road, a path of greening twigs nourishing

nothing personal. Root stocks

    of the best grapes, balm

for the honeybee's bite, lyme's flea—

    money chimes in the community bowl,

with patience I can sit on this bench

and wait for the ironworks of a previous century

    to reverse themselves, or I can lie in the grass,

vision the airplane's scatter-lit

    hallway, the descent

only a little shaky

    like the trouble between art and life rolling you out

onto an unpainted landscape,

the unbelted intoxication of travel   unstable as a chemical's twisted briar

medicine or drug   licit or illicit

or afterimage

time to move along

it's pathos time

dodge a supreme fear

pathos—

Patience was crowding anxiety

Patience's gentle tongue was breaking a bone,

while the twin and drone
to be patient with

hovered over

our uncharted, rimless wants,

rictus a slit vowel—

La vida,
a mess of dominoes
face down.

I am a pilot light

desiring more recognition,

I suck grass
to the dead inside.

The sleep aid cd & Hippocratic oath   mixed up good

in the cocktail of my head   spoken into like commerce's cavity,

cavity or skylight   opening to the early spring blossoms

in the airless baggage claim

SANCHEZ in stencil font
stitched to my desert fatigues

holding luggage   looking for someone to pick me up

I can be both
life-charged and dead
in consecutive units,

exited to like

turnpike rest stop's   promisingly lit

pagoda, a respite   for the humans stopping and returning, the humans predicating,

a human is someone
who has wandered in from the desert.

I am patience in a substance clothed.

truly a creepy troll
truly a creepy troll

a human is the one
continuing to close
Christ's eyes
on the great crucifixes

wagering will there   now be some inevitable progress.   In a tone pour,

the erotics of the electronics   swelling the house
and trailing to the sidewalk,

        skip to sound

a harrowing to go, a darned patch

A soft fontanel
a warm harm
a human

        does nothing

unusual, forgetting the euphoria
of human potential

is human potential

wanting more tools to form the mind.   Rest, stop, a human is go
stopping and returning,

a practice   a human is someone
to pick you up

a human is someone to hone
in a human's   long-held   desire to vanish   in a crowd or x-ed
out void of others,   in mass human's estranging light.

Experiments in Patience II

Family more
than genetics
and laundry

sweep the earth
in your
cemetery slippers

one foot slipping out

My Mother Moved My Architect

My mother moved
my architect
cutting out newspaper clippings
making the life-long collage
had I sense
I would have
papered the hallways with
instead it is an ephemeral art

a flaxen gene
her left shoulder
out of its socket

will remain that way
rest of days unto nights

what is mentally important

my mother moved my architect
I do not forget
unworn enormous straw hats having gone up in fire
butter churn, too,
a drummer drumming

differently in the hallway all years lead up the stairs
the lingerie

drying on the stairwell
the gait
got the girl in it

The Depression was in the Depression glass

the Carnival plate poised in the window
to seal the light said look

close to see your face

look in the face of your mother
giving way to continuance

redwolfing each nasal fold
and the pearly restitch   in the forehead   what happened there

my mother made
my amazon stockings

made my word order
accordian back   through the binoculars

the woody tendrils of the wisteria
a delicacy on the white pickets
sharpening up   the honeybee riding on that futurity

once my mother's face
spoke it said   let's tear up
our birth certificates and be transubstantiated

make of this world
a planetarium,   ultradense,

what the Big Dipper said to the Little Dipper:

my burial plans include   a new species but first

scatter my ashes
over the grave of your father
be sure to get the right grave
cemetery folks will tell you
this is illegal so do it at night

Midsummer my preference. Box turtle
so still as to look
dead in the middle of the lake.

If one could imagine
a mother between two swans.

Pomegranate   persimmons   shimmering trail of snail
copper nail in the earthen
dank shed
The miscellany began   the perplexity

                                              this drawer
                                              is for kitchen
                                              scissors

peel a grape for a glass eye
bleach kills mildew

toothpaste if no bleach
a kindness brought the pie

I do think at one point
as a woken child I saw
Bonnie and Clyde's' car
sleek and perfect   I then understood

God-speed
and if there were any morals I would take Thoreau's

I do not know how the coins got tossed up like that
to fall where they did.

nor the golden piss

      made sheerest.   relieved from a nude.

Look into your mother's face
fount yourself there

forget redemption.
If you want softness, wash your hair in rainwater.

If you crave guidance,
be Virgil to the Dante: *you didn't act this way in the other pit.*

My mother moved my architect
bade fair
she slipped the bolt
upright
like the great sea chest
none of us
had ever seen open

My mother moved my architect
she made it pump and eat

She made this lake
where I come to

over-identify with the dead and call

Dear Echo to my echo,

She made me nude —sheer— and nude again
She made it interesting right up to the end

So that
I have to think what is with

these two heads blurred and blended, this veil
not seen back through

Tail lights,
white gloves with the green stain

as you entered the sunless woods
best to keep the road a little feral where the color is

      and your world part dust
fed and unkilled   I am not through
being a poet or a being

What fallen ash
is the power to live

what pituitary
is the grace to keep
doing so

and what good
is temporary measure—

did you say thank you   and were you   thanking

Experiments in Patience III

the speaking machine sits there listening.

a pit and a dungeon.   somebody is not going

to make it in time, but will see you later.

a promissory.

out the window summer voices of children herded

by volunteers.   see you in ten.

how 'bout never?

how does never

sound?

a frayed stylus

brushes the worn-out record's

subcutaneous enormities.

look we've all heard this a million times.

graveyard boots

outside a white shed.

      I love you

beside a small red plastic fork.

    sag drags and falls,

Tuscaloosa   greyhound

there are those

who sit in your forever   travelling relics

to escape   the box stores

crows sweep to   typo
                            sky

[a drawbridge]

see you.   I love you,

but it spills

Peace

It fell

    of noon

      weather-like

as in

    a poem the

sudden action of a single word

    you know

      people,

        once you tell them something

          they start talking

[Peace]

smells of sweat deep
in sport-full fields
eyes opened and were thrilled or soothed and sustained
we had won
cars passed along streets in bright difference or decay

[Peace]

in argument context shivers the trigger words
before munitions, oil extracted from the cotton
makes the town smell sweet
no corpus, only body's eidolon
marijuana scented hush of the glove compartment
in your device, a person spies the bridge in flames then flees
so old school, the photo in its bath

[Peace]

contrary to history, to war's punctuations
the almost dripping popsicle held from the body
on the heat-buckled sidewalk, earth's
involuntary memory to descend and ascend,
the round. the blue.
to begin all over again.

4th

of July

bagpipes   big mad Hitchcockian crows

siren   families striding   hurrying

want a whole lot of love   sings the Joplin

mimic   white birch   willow swings   pollen

the cars in shade

way way down gonna give you my love

staying in the house

the crows outside are winning

car door   a muffled crowd gasp   wheels at the top of the sky

and waits

the night sky's visuals

called   "Untamed Retribution"   and "Rain Fire"

an objective   sincerity   the war does not space itself

two teenage   girls at the screen   with the sun in their eyes

all day   time takes

all the time   bright canisters in the culverts   girls read

hills of it

day-long trash truck heads down our street

what a big

engine   emergency brake

distance between   telephone pole and queen palm's trunk

smoke loops   from back of the house to front

leaves no signet   in cloud   sidewalk's scalding path

'neath county's ripe

corn table

globe's eggshell

for romance   the girls layer their tears back into their skin

many dawns   the boys waving

bends

air crosses clouds in hot nets

increasing   the local tenor's uprightness

fumes exhume

the crowd stands open-mouthed

heads lifted

you
you
you
you
you
and
you
send me

smoke falls through each head of hair

to each ear's

                size and limit

                                        love

sound-chamber'd

moon's

far off

place

[Peace]

death is to be entered backwards
the necessary condition, a partial vision
at my father's funeral, a blind field
the flag taken from over the casket
folded into a triangle, handed to us
throughout "the reception"
a boy eyes a pizza slice
on a white paper plate

Opened

FOR GABRIELLE GIFFORDS

So it was like sleep and waking, sleep and

fraud on my   Visa, sleep

                          California

waiting out radioactive plume,

and today another

trying card

in Miami
Winn Dixie

                        did they want groceries

or did they want cash, sleep

 Freeway sign said   take Lucky Drive

to bypass

bank robbery in shopping mall

so that's where

                                the two bullets went through.

What sphinx pushes up out the fog in the parking lot

turning each

upon each

our moral imaginations. If it's a gun law,

        this tragedy will pull through.

And what was there to   and did she

see, gritty blue sink of desert night sky   with her

off to the side like a wonder, or

your basic hospital room, sleep,

          a solitary male nurse, a husband.

Here we pour a new layer, visible

for all to see how we want
      to be as transparent as possible,

    but remain gradient,

dangerous when once it was them,

          an error, a horror now that it is

What are we to the man

who attacked the gunman

as he started to reload, a constituency?

Ducks

in the arcade stir a glassy water, sleep, amplify

Gun with cord tied to it so no one will take it

The little girl with a hole in her chest

first girl player to play

in the middle leagues

Gritty blue sunken—shame— as if the desert

could hiss, fold,

The six dead behind her eyelids.   Leave them open,

let us place no more constraints on the eyes of the dead,

illegible cross-outs turned inward,

searching themselves to escape

like figures met in a dream,

she is walking down the hall with a shopping cart

              —Never and always

a back to the door—   Whose side—

  Once she appears again,

    but they won't show her to us

 at her husband's launch of four spacewalks

to install the alpha magnetic spectrometer   It will take all four walks

         to sift, sleep

through cosmic rays

to define the origin of the universe, though

                by now, that plays a minor key.

     It could be plutonium, it could be uranium,

we just don't know.

              A radioactive plume

to drift over California Friday by noon   a shadow of cloud on the stream

Crows that range and radiate

    from cloud to tumbling cloud

     And what will she say

privately   and what will she say

              in that language of our conviction.

This tragedy will pull through,

and will stand by you tomorrow.

It isn't really heavily radiated water.

How one eye keeps one eye

on a deep and bitter thing.

late democracy

we the undersigned understand then the green of the meadow

has turned to

you who are not my body I vow to you
my resemblance

unequal in value and significance to string my verbal chain:

just let me go out swilling whiskey in the hill country

as imagined and planned.

         who wants to sit around

         worrying about

         third party ads

         on the site

where she and he who is one of them

      (sweet secret green of the yellow)

troll.   they are going to steal my identity:

        metaphysic of a clicking bloom, lotus cup

[Peace]

halftone of a couple in a four poster
who left their breath together
or took too much
white clapboard   distant city
her vagina his cock slack in the cosmological moisture
Christ gets so misquoted
once they put the Latin in him
looking out of the picture wanting nothing

[Peace]

if a no more one without the other
could peace and war be a co-presence
peace and war a co-presence
one hand holding another
a metaphysics their separateness a reality
one can no longer touch? we flock to, inflate
death's impatiences

Plath and Sexton

there should have been a third
my friends and I

to not feel so incomprehensible
we were carrying your dead books

we were washed in the blood of them
but we were wanting one more

for a while we tried Artaud's "all writing is shit all writers are pigs"

our clubhouse   language   death   war   music   fireflies for an opera

we were thinking a lot about the feminine
we were putting our feminine in a suitcase

and waiting for

caution tape

hyperlinks to take us to
the tulip scape   the blue blazer scape

infinity's integument
undoing

pageboy, if you hold on, we could all be the
third, and you, the task
of our young life,   strangely exhilarated

Monday Morning

everything was on sale   the pop music was under the heat lamps

and the spectacle was on the television

and the television was in the spectacle

the life that is at least ¾ automatism   said to the life

that isn't   just look

at the great big burden of you   quit mail   quit mail

Beyoncé   (Beyoncé put a ring on it check it out youtube)

try to live as though it were morning,   said Nietzsche

can we show off the backbends in the yoga class   and still progress

that is a very optimistic statement of Nietzsche's

it was morning and all the white guilt got balled up

and tossed through the sky then landed back

into the white guilt which had made   a very good deal   with the white privilege and the light through the burnt-out leaf pattern   in the curtain fabric

fell to the hands spread-eagle   on the yoga mat   pushing hard

one friend called and said "here we are"   and I said   "here we are"

and the hand picked up the garden hose curled in the calla lilies

drips of water in the copper snout   and giovanni called and said it never

occurred to me there WOULDN'T   be a black president why is everyone calling me

to congratulate   ME   I didn't do a thing   I know a lot of black people

with good jobs   look there's one   says giovanni   with a bad cold

who was born after the Civil Rights Movement   so I point that   out to her

and she says yeah right   my last cousin not in prison just went to prison

nothing's over   so I look at my hand no longer spread on the yoga mat

same hand that slapped hands wiped up shit stacked money cut the vegetables

and filled in the dot   *Cinderella, Camelot*   the white guilt said to the white guilt

don't you even try to feel better now   you still have to

wake up in the morning and live as though it were morning

you can give yourself a little release more breath a very large exhale through the mouth

you done good girl   you can go to the grocery store   you can look

into the black faces   you encounter   everywhere in all the jobs

good and bad and they look back at you   a little different now

you can't say what it is   you can't describe it

but you can observe it   if you can stay aware long enough   every morning

it is the morning you can try to live   as though it were morning

the ghost wars   whispering to the ghost wars   their Miranda rights

the white privilege starting the car   trying out the back seat

knuckle bone   flat palm   pinkie   finger wide

here we are   here we are

try to live as though it were morning

light on the hands   spread eagle   breathe and the white guilt said   hold   hold

Trying to Write a Poem About Gandhi

I.

The future leaves roses on the bed

for the long stretch of the waker

at the window left to pull

the day around.   History props up and swarms a lot of time.

Wonder will he walk back.   Should we still run to keep up with him.

Fingers quick to thread the spinning wheel.

A dizziness in the face

of a social machine.

      Silver, infinitesimal motes   shine lift and hover-cloud

I shake out the dryer's lint drawer

             into garage air— *satyagraha,*

no power over the soul

the body suffers

II.

A silver pocket watch pinned to a loincloth

        Better to hand wash

In past and in future   Postmodernism's gone all artisan

        motes swirling up into stale garage air

Open door   to let it   drift out   spread into wisteria's tresses

        ahimsa,

   a matter not of the intellect

   but of the heart

III.

Beloved figures die

        then stop and loop

to pixelate,

a history sweeps and fells the picture field.   In uppermost

loamy branches of the giant oak

sit Thoreau, Tolstoy, Ruskin, Emerson and Carlye.

Shining down their texts.

Unorthodox social moralists of the 19th century

still trying to freeze hell.

Many leafy wandering past participles in my neighborhood alone.

Also one assault rifle, a shotgun, two Glock pistols

one tactical armored vest   How do I know this   several gas masks

one child's ballistic leggings   ballistic helmet

one known pedophile

Best to try not to wish anyone

dead, think John Berryman, "I woke up, and I had not murdered anyone,"

before I turn back to the dryer, thinking why think   or try to be like Marx

who said at the end of his life, I am not a Marxist.

That's my girl's lost blue sweater hung on the fencepost.

Best to think of even nuisances

in your inbox

       as pilgrims on earth, immortal spirits on probation.

IV.

How to make of one's garden a Tolstoy Farm.

And be chief magistrate, prime minister,

main teacher, chief baker, chief sanitary inspector

of a modest magnetic field produced by electric currents in earth's outer core, on earth's

crust primarily quartz (silicon dioxide) and other silicates like feldspar.

One too bright day, here comes Manu and Abha.

Manu—grandniece, and Abha—wife of grandnephew—

Gandhi's "girls" and "walking sticks," his hands

on their shoulders as he walked everywhere with them toward the end.

Poverty easy   but chastity eludes
and means

       funny sleeping arrangements—

younger and younger naked girls to sleep

beside

to "maintain" chastity

brahmcharya,

elimination of all desire
in the face of temptation

Accept the body!
You pussy,   picture field says dropping down

great thinkers or/
scheming demotic despots it's a thin line
to undo and silly
to be an apologist for a pacifist

Dale Carnegie   ☒ friend

Madame Blavatsky   ☒ friend

Why think
God doesn't like
        pussies, cocks, girls, Gandhis   all together
well, you'd have to ask the girls,
and later

It's a subrosa geological planet, with shifting hot mantels of tectonics,
someone should tell Einstein—
even though it's too late—who said,
"Future generations will hardly grasp that
such a man as this walked upon the earth."

Palm fronds for shade.

                    Basil, peppers, early tomatoes here.

Strawberries under chicken wire to frustrate deer.

In the garden, motes and mites,
                             all waxes and wanes
in shadows' leafy deep sea ocularity.

The future drags and drifts and lifts   traces of argon, carbon dioxide and water,
sun's majestic past and impending

life. "You cannot hope to wake anyone who isn't fully asleep"

              he said

"you cannot wake those who are *pretending* sleep"

Tenderness of the Dove

tender or tinder   put me in one   a box

with velvet lining

stay the glove

to warm the hand

quivering masterfully the fishes etched in lime

downriver, thick with stream

it was too quiet to hear the ringing

and yet we wed   a changeling   to a trifling

a red sweater   was my love   a color rinsed my hair

a guitar

we all gave out   playing

Toughness of the Serpent

I think maybe we should take out 10 or 12 of them

      just to show that we are serious, says E. D. Nixon to MLK.

Montgomery's steam fallen into leafiness, warm midnight temper

            of faucet water. Transfigurative green Cadillac

of one Mrs. A. W. West

         catching the dew in her carport.

Dreaming-in-waking   blood brotherhood of those tried to live paradise

            buses empty

              in the recessive spaces.

MLK really tired at this point.

Wonder what he's got on his mental sky.

         Moon yellow scorch of the morning iron, serene, serene

A Healing for Little Walter

One day we were just lying around trying to key the sound.

Trying to sound the wound, make it bend, loop it through.

Fishbone scar let loose from the forehead,

swim upriver, what touch is to someone alone.

We brought melon and honey, cheap liquor for the task. Gold fill. Gold leaf fill.

Sought sound of a man born in the Crossroads, thirty miles

south, four-corner out near Marksville, Louisiana.

Marksville, Louisiana, with its French signs.

Sound if you wait twelve o'clock a black cat.

Sound if tall man with red eyes appears all you see is red.

Every time you open your mouth it's red.

What flesh is to bone.

That boy has a nice tone.

Spit easing down

a child's toy come rain. Fish fell from the sky in Marksville, 1947.

Fish fell. We were just lying around trying to key the sound.

Eventually a bone went straight to the forehead.

Small 10-hole Hohner Marine Band harmonica then cheapo harmonica

brought to the brink on one easily overloaded, state-owned, then state-discarded,

public address amplifier.

Sound that removed our heads from our back-sides, sound

we could lay in, drape, then pour its honey onto

and glisten with, the spider web left at the dark Apollo.

Marksville population 5,537

at 2000 census, total area 4.1 square miles, of which

10.6 km² is land, 0.24%, water.

Where once was the Crossroads.

Marksville, Louisiana with its French signs.

Let us break down the farm of Louis Leviage on Drupines Road.

Knock on the door of the shotgun shack beside.

Death our greatest front man.

That and a bullet-shaped microphone.

The humble mouth organ.

Once harmonica 25 cents after Little Walter 10 dollar.

Today even jackhammer got the juke

cracking up pipeline breaking through wall into sun again.

Instrument saying to its player, thanks man, thanks Marion Walter Jacobs.

What flesh is to bone you must pass to pass through.

Sprinkle sachet powders down deep personal valleys.

Breaking through wall into sun again

Tina knew how to Turn and Run.

Carla got the ropy veins.

Knocking on the door of the shotgun shack beside.

What flesh is to bone.

Every time you open your mouth it's red.

What he did, he took advantage of himself being himself, on himself, you know?

Sashay Little Walter.

What flesh is to bone.

High rolling, passing through.

Liquor golden. Knife shut. Fist pulled back and stuck into pocket.

Head from your backside. Forehead smoothed. Gold fill. Gold leaf fill.

That isn't Death in the middle that's a minor stream.

A tall man with red eyes appears all you see is red.

That isn't breath on the downside that's another minor stream.

That boy has a nice tone.

A public address amplifier thereby shall we have increase of the light.

Small 10-hole Hohner Marine band harmonica

cheapo harmonica then Little Walter

holding a black cat before a man with a white cane.

Fish fell. Four corners spread wide open. Stab wounds in the dirt.

Knocking on the door of the shotgun shack beside. Gold fill. Gold leaf fill.

Carla and Tina rose and fell

Tina still rising.

A blue peal bent so far back it's red.

Little Walter, beasts looking solemn at you

from the other side.

Tina still rising.

Turn and Run.

Gold fill,

Gold leaf fill.

Fishbone thereby shall we see the light.

A silver pickup at the yellow end.

Like gold into scar

a twister in the skull.

    Fish scales

        rising in the tub

           and the river.

A beast's molecular

snore and drone

on the other shore.

Carla rising

running with Tina.

A masterhood

that bet

you missed a note

and grooved thereby.

Now a carven turkey

once a wild hoot

a harmonica clung to

and fell from.

Carla rising running with Tina.

What he did.

Like gold into scar a twister in the skull.

Thank you, man.

Beast looking solemn at the sun shown up for supper.

Knives lifting the four corners

shook out chains molt to moebis a pierce into the blueness.

Turn, and Run.

Cetripedal, centripetal.

Gold fill, gold leaf fill.

Crying and wailing with our toy harmonicas

in a space gone unbolt into

a blueness sucking in the sun

sun on the liquor golden

sun down the farm

sun on the door of the shotgun

your mouth it's red

to bone.

to bone.

sun on the spit easing down.

                pipeline through wall.

            every time you open

            instrument saying

            thereby shall we

            someone alone

            One day

            sun down deep

            what flesh

            fell from

break down

the

forehead

        the

        sky

every time

touch is

day

you open your mouth

pass through

A hatchet with which to chop at the frozen seas inside us

to wake to winter   in the coming out of the time of year

when they release

the masterpieces,

                        but to be still in the other night.

            some drown in movies.

some prefer the unfinished

ungovernable recital,

                a mystical ecology

            where one dies in a camp,

    or rolls out with the dice

            on the sidewalk among boys with

cardboard shields

                        and plays dead in white crinoline.

what if paradise was only lifting the veil to flirt.

no one perfect, but perfection inserts

us so, Pascal

thinks a God in his pocket.

what if paradise meant walking

on the ground of our self estrangement,

and the veil of our gaze

an unsteady balm

was not what we saw through

but were,   twisting, untwisting—

do you believe.   we were never strictly servants.

VII.
NEXT

borderlands

Late flies large as nearly extinct black bees

burrow in wisteria

when the desert has all the carcasses

Flies grow L's for legs

the world often barely perceptible, its sometime sugary smell

a rustic divination, a chainlink

Debt builds

credit,

the envelopes tower on the kitchen counter

tilt day's movement from spring to

summer, when at last there is time, huge delivered cubes of it

to open all newspapers shoved under couch, tape some

on walls, make links

with a red Sharpie

and still I cannot learn

our kingdom its cages

At Rite Aid: Infinite Shine 2 Lacquer nail polish

named Withstands Test of Thyme

an aqua transbluent sage, nice

Women in sundresses, shirtless men, fish trapped

by ecstatic children brown, white

carrying magenta-haired dolls into river

sky blue remote bot drones

Balancing red snapper arranged on a plate, signature

cocktails, browser, dowser,

bitching on my vacay, I ride tidal galaxy in gulf whitecaps

I have time to think

how does one

make of time

a servant

    not the other way around—when there is nothing to do one can

discern a divine intervention from an ambrosial urban myth

        it is an extremely

        advanced yoga pose

to enact

such a dimension of

     "here I am" and "there are

     others" above the Pacific, pelicans in military formation

make a feathered V, I say a few words

into an abandoned silo

I say "citizen of the world"

up to blown sky—

                I say welcome to our infinite, unmerciful, eternal estrangement, home

to the girl from Oaxaca crossed over

a placenta's swell
                           > she says this partnership is not working out
a purple martin in deleafed tree

whenever I say I it sounds extrajudicial,

the fine sprays of misunderstood words also say

check out shelf with local honey

it will help you

breathe better

and be dreamful companion

to polyglot strangers who built our republic,

their strolling, ghostly greenish speckled shade cast under oaks

already a chainlink

hitch to her stride

        Radio says

           put saucer of sugar water out   if you see a weak black bee

     And if there is no place

    to park the car

  why did you get in it

I wonder if courage in one world

      can create an expanse in another

           Is it akin to lovers   who are alive in each other?

Pushing my cart past shelves

the grocery aisle says sea salt

is a sorryass hygienic tragedy

When I check out, the robot thanks me for doing its work

I say we're still alive in a polite tone

In the morning the river is busy

dividing an uncracked code

Everlasting

In the Next Next World

That sound Arvo Pärt does with one piano note

stars split, fade, wander

in cosmic expansion—

First responder's genesis and torch of

metadatacrunch tumbling in a

burnt and weedy churchyard

equal parts Lethe and lithe—

Grass, is it hollow, hallow

to wake no longer among

mortals? The woman her dress flowered

from a blown ceiling silver-rosed—

Flat plasm's

archangel coming clear out

of sheetrock and screen

shield and spear in hand

let us do all the cooking

if she will lead the pack, remember the route, read the waters—

After the great fire we

tread river's late cream and flare.

We woke in a city.

Where who slew us into portions

on a block out of earth

gathered our limbs

and we were allowed to continue

unhunted. If "if" is the one word one is given with God

to explain how one survived.

Oh. Ah. Siren,

white cockatoo

meets deep

blue.

Fog. Pour ammonia

on coyote

scat.

Humans Done Standing along
Abundant Endless Cross Streets

when can we   lift off a redacted divinity

a lava geode cut into cubes   creation

    a black pearl slipped from its necklace

      darkness flutes a trail

holes in the paper   the four winds blow through

    betafish circles   its bowl conjuring silver,

backflipping   spatial inequities my-hand-to-eye   learning difference

  calla lilies rim the lake

     my teeth, these canines!

I was of a space-faring species who loved the rill of no gravity

when water was spotted

     extending from telescopes seen as from a great distance

such was the sea, my friends' green cards tossed

grew choppy, presumptive,   wishful,   that word *friend*s

who are not   grateful not to work   in sunken ponds under strung

light my dialectic my diaspora my who is going to give me a diamond ring thing

  I am cognitively advanced in milliseconds

or I am crowd sourced and derivative

    on a passing train

Yellow forces the acacia   hollow eucalyptus twilight

    the kind farm the swollen island

        of gold chains I wrap around others' ankles

black ankle monitor   a house arrest   for my wild and rueless child

 my stupid stupid

    stupid leaders

I abandon them here

in my oppressor's language on my suppressor tongue

beneath the inertia of my garments the aphasia

of a half-read T-shirt's   passerby on a city street

gone country road where leaves form

yellow windrows

or tumble down the dark

macadam. What is saying my benevolence? Space

buildings   cars   how close

hostility's slow drag

"peace" "peace" "hate" hated   the words throw back

my head   feels screwed-on, sidejacked

in brain's midspout,   clouds   sky.

Where was I going

What backscattered metamorphosis?

Cattails weeds   aloe   paper rope shadow   broken pickets

splinter   the mid-day galaxies   the graves

I've stood at,   before,   and think I've seen

a start in the peripheral

new ortho legs of a coming

sphere scrape grid of how, when

Thank You for the Afterlight

the yellow tinged with cyan   primal coat

   the gingerale,   a mother figure   at first   all face

      the existence that is   a continuance

and extinction, a malted or smoothie

    of the brain freeze, long spinal stretch, and ice age of knowing you, Creator

rile and denial   of the human animal

    buzz saw and honeybee of our correspondence

I reacted to

not unregretfully,   it was

            carried back

       unsigned   I am

writing you   no more

often lies run

a little backwards

in this missive oblivion

where synapse thinks it saw a spirit

equators shiver

across to one another

golden tanager and cock-of-the-block

roareth   in the revolution

on the earth's surface   I know

moment to moment   half

to one third of all thought

is cat vomit really in the middle of the night

while it was supposed to be medicinal

to eat the grass   this bristly

prelapsarian keyhole of a hut where my finger

 lingers   as you   row by

  is that all

to perception   You are like

privileged Ivy League

assessing me   I am

another

white thing

    that little eggshell still stuck on my blouse

I cracked out of you I see that now

   in this skirt rose-splashed, bereft of aura

I love my tiny part Neanderthal DNA

   left, cast-off I go bootless into lyric structures

landfill's clear containers

There may have been someone who loved you

more than you loved saving

    that's how you got on this road

and so disfigured

  in land, in word

    standing like a crucifix on a porch while the cars go by

Where   to put   last century's   threadbare Sunday   dress with arms uplift

and begin   to strut a bit

between star and tar

    Celestial nest, also like stress, hormone, breathing with high peaks

skeletal sensory too, combustible planetarium,

    an interstitial musculature where

ceiling angels peel and flake a weather

turned glassy in which you

    are the shaken narrator   bundled up

taking a few trips   around the block, running one loose hand over

    the increasingly familiar hedges

     For what have you done

   that so many   run to surround and warm

you, a boy and girl so porous with the air,

    lunar, earthly, I try very hard to never close the parenthesis on you,

  it's one way to atone

    for perhaps you are just swimming

slowly   to another scribe waiting

    sort of perpendicularly   in the lake   near the shore

maybe that's what

     time is

under shaded oak tree's   co-substantiates

the numbers of the house   we come to find

all the while   realism's steady message—

  someone really loves someone   and then doesn't—

someone almost reads a name

  your sinister subtraction   these fits and starts get chalked

 then smudged away

into grey otherworldly cloud

 on sidewalk's cracked bodice

despite great gusts of pressure

When Lie Goes Live

The wind in the trees shuffle a sonic ephemera
under which to feel stable

    An hour spent half-seeing stone soldiers in the plaza

In other centuries was it harder to tell
      perception from paranoia
                dissociation?

    One false fall yellows the leaves all the way to the parking lot

Cheekbones rent a helmet, an odd bend to a branch

     Summer's last tiger lilies deepen, I dreamed my husband

went to war last night, he would never

dream that of me

The actuality of our malfunctioning
disharmonies, steadily,

slowly the paper mache statue of liberty

gets wheeled out to the baseball field
for the star-spangled, and falls
sidelong, and we laugh

but affectionately. I like a man
leaning into white stucco
smoking his pack's last cigarette

unknown to the drone,
the surveillance camera's turned back on itself

an installation site-specific, the soft focus of his eyes
turning to me while I hang on

to my near empty notebook's   low wide white noise

Most streets I sense a solid escape another death

a rupture along each page's glue

Pieces of what people say

get repeated internationally

If they catch on long enough

above the people   sitting disinterestedly

mute in a park

The man who went to war
going AWOL by the alarm clock
a pork stew in the
slow cooker

ham hock for the feds
who wouldn't know
what to do with a ham hock, shake or consume

so tired of talking now
though I can't begin

I don't know how I could feed you

The Long Marriage

If it is true that I, you, don't exist but we are in it

for the eternity, for the once

in the pink-orange blazing dawn I put on

your black underwear.

Doing there,   in my drawer,

stunned/pleased at the hip-fit,

years to a bus   you jumped out of

in your duct-taped boots   (there was snow),

you were so happy to be coming to see me

I saw you from the window's

vectored frost,   a brown feathery

hen, here to roost, though you

were the male.   Now the white birch drifts

a thousand motes   back into the house

to eat off our dust and fly.

We sire and wench,   harmony and ash

   until conversation, consumption,

   interrogation, and the small back of the sweet talk

become so paradisical, primitive, warped

   I fall into the lace of your gutter,

pretty nice there,

   and we have to wire prose into the talk to get the poem,

to get the rope that runs long and free

   out the cave. Mastodon-like to crawl on all fours to birth

some intelligibles.

   Got a grease fire in the kitchen for a long time coming.

   Couples forming a rustling seriality

up city hall's granite steps'

nightlong cormorant moon, 20 pairs of black underwear in a superbag be-lit with break

of dawn's exalt

as when media hyper-glosses our lives but not as bad

as your mom and dad, and we think of

our dreams with their heterodoxy and did I tell you mine or dream it

the lava-like tar

congealing into blue-black bubbles in asphalt

we could pop with each step.

Sissy Spacek and Martin Sheen in the movie of our first

date both so young all they could do was kick thoughtlessly at the dirt

and kill everyone in their wake

but us. Spacek's short shorts her child-like, almost woman-like

legs. Sheen's cigarette pack folded back into the sleeve of his T-shirt,

we rose/stumble/found each

other's hands up the aisle pitch dark

and stood before the turn lights

turning jade green water. If anoit is a drop of oil

on our foreheads,   if one by one alteration finds,

we toss our hair down a tower

for longer arousal. We want to be seen in the eyes of the government.

If marriage is Empire's locket

we get in bed like students to its sheets

though we hate the acquisition and the light moves.

How many instances of unity feel more like

bicycles attached to cars.

But that was your dream.

I get on the bus going nowhere in particular,

sit in sun for the warm.

The bus heaves sideways before lurching down our

street crowded (it is Wednesday) with the Episcopalian's AA meeting's

cars, each shining, obediently

parked. Luck, its inexact clarity.

Soft as tracing paper the house lay

loose linoleum,

carpet, tile and oak for surfaces

to pace, parse, backtrack.

If this is the hallway

where a lumbering tiger with stitches mends itself and runs.

We cannot occupy it absolutely, ion, eon.

If this is the vertigo of another.

One song alone, one spinet,

many breezes, firmament, and water.

The psalm and plasm in the particulars

of the jungle where we walk to see it snow.

If we are so angry.

If we are so happy.

If no eye contact. The wind tears hard at it.

Preparing one's consciousness for the avatar

Was a rare sun   its sudden mouths,   shrugs and voices.

A birth   a sleep   a forgetting   a God

or scientist   or brain.   Or when in   mind or on a freeway   a red/orange sign

drops down   says

do not neglect, nor demonize   the demons.   The lice are feasting.

Drafts, computations,   clean for more   space, rid unnecessary surfaces

bottled water   Agua pura, sabor perfecto.

Avatar, atavistic   just a brief, lettristic shuffle   *avatar* chiefly Hindi,

manifestation   of a deity   or released soul   in bodily form

on earth   (*are you? maybe, don't flatter me*)   from the Sanskrit

ava "down" + tar "to cross,"

and atavistic   origin 19th century (*in your dreams*) from the Latin

atavus "forefather" via French

atavisme. Frankenstein   bewildered   at his limp or rising member still a little angry   re: parlor game   his cheek   tingles   nuzzles and buries

itself   in verdant marl.   World welcomes more   world   in sun

the young muscled   amputee in basketball shorts   heading cheerfully,

quickly to the ferry.   *Don't stir*

                         the trash,

                    writes Sappho.

            It's you and I   in pursuit   counter-pursuit,

in the long epiphany   of having a face.   Was it 16th century—

to simulate rain—water spray   was released over   mechanical dolls

sent flying near the masterpieces— Or was that you   who were tired

                              of not being

                         and so began   calling for help?

                         If I   were a mothering belly

                         would I

heave or contract   out your   tangled, wired tissues   a silkworm

cocoon,   put your head at my feet   and we'll pretend.

You would not think it is this young Russian

who wants us all to live forever. Walking earth down

to basalt, shale, slate.

Sea-roaring is the blood

in sparrows of the Holy Ghost

a ting, ting in bell tower.

Maritime, lorikeet, sleet. Dimitry Itskov

(pale yellow Borelli blazer,

rose-gold watch, 32, a mild-mannered, internet billionaire)

is non-plussed, sweet of face

which someone

(David Hanson, of Hanson Robotics) in Plano, Texas,

is duplicating, carefully,

paused above a tiny haired brush   for the eyelids   in the *Times*.

36 motors to reproduce facial expressions and voice.

"No more world hunger," says Dimitry Itskov. At least for you. While others are always hungry. So some refrigerators   will have to stay, some sent to dump

in silver or white array—look in, look away.

How to figure   when to leave the body

summer's blue jay   calling   caw caw caw   quick-diving down to peck

the calico/tortoise mix, who waits so stoic, still. Only

to pounce later.   Do you play cat   or bird?   Blue jays lift and spin,

graze the sheet on the line,   turn

into a tumescent   sub-group, the organs of our fancy...

                                        Felonies and phantoms

                        of DNA   like sharp notes

                                cleared   of choir

                    while floats a

yellow post-it,   postage size,   cropped fabric/memory   of my dead

father's blue/grey   wet plaid swim trunks—   a flash—

The burled hand-rest   at the end   of the burnt stairway—

Time to clean, to clean and polish, the figures and friends

are coming over, the ones   who read, command   and trail us,

hello canary,   hello reptile,

parrot   brother   sister   and oh wow,   is that you celebrity?   and child.

If you don't see them now you

will soon—no turning back—

they are mostly atavistic,   powerful in what

they get us to look like, do and say.   At least you—still in production—don't

have to sleep next to them,   or wake up and wing it—

The wind bellows and rattles the house.

Ice, ice drops another cube.   Tiny tinny birdsong.

Wild red fox   purple zinnia   stone pelican   raven.

The celebrities scrub themselves down to the shine.

My mother who is now speaking

in sentences of no more than four words

reclines on the armchair

to watch

like a bony glamorous cheetah,   an unwrinkled sleeve   stilled

in the complementary then analogous

color theory of the room, the

debris box they are taking away

a week from Friday.   One of the figures

has died.   And jumped into the debris box.

One of the figures   trailing the friends.   Delete, clean.

Old sound of empty chimney when wind dips down

into sudden clang.   Is that you again— gathering yourself, hiding, expansive in

the silence   after sound?   Ok,   I will give you my childhood neighbor who sat in the backyard painting her china plates,

her dyed black hair   done up in a knot—

Breasts loose in a housedress.   Her wondrous teats

falling over her waist   above the astonishingly small petals

she is painting on the plates   with tiny haired brushes.

The rotting garage behind her.   And what's this?

Cloudy afterimage of myself and cousin   in her upstairs bed her

funeral night? Cool, old, dark, empty house.

Fooling around in riverbank's low grasses

the day before? The same

cousin, at least.

                                                            Blue palette extending

                        beyond sky over windless   sidewalks that tilt and buckle

at most tree-rooted spots. I know this way

     like I have trudged it all along

every new street.   Immortality,   if you are coming,   you are

310

the last figure off the boat.   I am the one   who gently pushes the boat

away, and wishes you well,   the friends and figures slowly extinguishing

then enlivening   the word love,   and the love in gone and ever.

And the boarded-up window

in the rotting garage,   and still no relief.   The palm tree that rises

through years then molts in wind storm   its deeply crevassed

bark canoes.   Black crow bringing in the wake,

soul made   to deflate, inflate

to transfer   like breath   to a summer hammock.   The neighbors lifting

chaise lounges in   thick smears of sun. Red nail polish fades

off the key used most. Windows

preferably high, clear

so puppet theatres of day

bring   cloud, tree   car, fence.   Some stranger

is getting in the front seat.   First one spindly leg and then the other.   Plump, liquefy, reconstitute. Hot light-rinsed light   where the celebrities

stand for   our smoothing of the images,

the labor of the evening out

of the images which works   to heal

the celebrities' carved faces

and bodies,   the frayed hoodies

they retreat to, scraped out images

of the cloaks and rags and rugs—

In imitation of prayer, palm meets palm,   our hands designed

to make a folio. The start of childhood is one folio

in which the family gathers to stand

as before a window, each individual so rarely pictured with the entire group,

unless it is a storm where one can point and pass,

evaporate as ghosts to sea.   Oh optometry,

hazel, mauve, ochre   low field of burning barn   across which one can holler a centering "amen" and "we shall live again" a species

    of rock and trace mineral,

of many marks and laughter.   These formations you will inherit just by

    staring us back in the face.

Canary, parrot, brother, sister, celebrity, child. Expenditure, skeins,

    who is Your Excellency?

Who your dissimulated author? I am sad under my sheets

    if you are amped tireless soldier.

[I am going to dissolve/then suture all this back inside me

    while in storm light drops the lantern.]

And why

is your Dmitry Itskov face painted so blue, so boy blue

if only to make us think death, or Thomas

Gainsborough's blue velveted boy,   boy on the brink

of childhood's end,

when so many imagine their deaths red,   or colorless, somehow more free—

antiphonal,

if you want to lift the blood that way. . .

          Of all my friends and figures

     I prefer the woman who walks   in the loosest way

down the conveyor belt, along the metronomes and mechanical dolls,

like one who prefers to not be there— had nothing to do with it—

does not want to   command or suggest,   only to go one's own way

through the   discordant   collective sweep.

          Most brains are not quite done,

     or have regions

          disturbed or blank, this area

     without synapse   shooting away

from itself— She's in one, looking for a place to stand

and wish for elsewhere and harmony,

a slow dangling of a branch   into black water that is a part

of how we, being 'round thee, forget to die?

And can drop anchor

into knowing   one another

through projecting expressions,   timbres, tones of voice

and even   clothing's   pale importance   then loud colors   though all this

dies down   when one is alone,   bearable days on end for some,

only a few hours for most—

Leagues of contagion   residual beauty   recorded, battered candlelight.

She's the kind   no one is the single file of.

You will come to see

these figures and join their ranks

perhaps? Eventually though later than we? Given your fuel,

your ability to last   be last.   I'll just stand

and wait in snow's   meandering   lost call, called back.

If we go down these stairs, the besotted government

of each continent,   village, and hut.

If we go up, the beginning

crevices of the infinity,   each step disappearing beneath

blooms and ducts   of a repatterning,

sun-struck sky. Gone this thing

of having two feet on the ground   unless they are

curled up in a chair   or tucked or

splayed out elsewhere. Gone the floors of polished jasper, wood and creak. We'll fly,

    imaginary, expenditure, skeins,   through gates of

        rust-stained bougainvillea   heart-breaking over the

    ringing in our ears   in the long division

        of our end's negation   and its annihiliation

shadow shadow shadow   follow follow—

Apologia

And so, I was human guilty

I had driven innumerable cars parallel, pumped gas,

poured Draino down toilet

Roundup along dandelions

and I had thought I could tell the truth,

in my worn and scarred golden Birkenstocks, and all fled

my berry-stained

hands, so when the solar flare from the wildfires' silicate particles

showered down onto my shoulders, which were bare, night-gowned,

pock-marked by various

cancers removed and

barnacles scraped, I long ago decided

after so much of my own enjoyment

I would just let the sun eat me,

my metabolic sugars rimmed with mucosa,

zygote, spermatozoa, fur, gif and ion the earth

a dog shaking us off like tics was an oft-reported theory

                    "Somehow the universe can be seen as one

                    natural disaster" was the molten ore

                    the earth spat back at me

Down the flamed blocks the "pop" "pop" "pop" of deindustrialization

                    Somehow still standing there, hauling my air purifier my HEPA filters

        walking back into work I was parasite,

            clinging to her meaningless heavens—poems—

        nitrogen dioxide

        nitrous oxides

        benzene

        aldehydes

brain ethanol

blood ethanol

carbon monoxide

slivered cinders fell into my

wanted to slide a garden hose down

throat for relief

the earth's hide a charred vellum

where I replicated, vision blurred,

navigating smoke with my lizard eye

       I had driven by lawns smoldering their cytotoxic activity,

       another chimney-as-tombstone unscratched,

       "flames fast as three football fields in 30 seconds"

polycyclic aromatic hydrocarbons

    "who lost their house wasn't you"

"was not your sister-in-law"

      doors not husks

an N-95 mask fell down your face   your body kept its outfits

"you drove through an afterlife and remained"

In the Department of Forget It We Won't Take Care of You

In the Institution of Regardless We'll Pay You

release of hydrogen cyanide became acquainted with

each chest's alveolar macrophage

The hungriest white egrets

flew at their maximum of 25 mph to better air,

to dip their beaks into luncheon at the lagoon

of the immense entropic morn-crowning

glory glory

still above water

earth

POEMS AS THEY APPEARED IN
ORIGINAL COLLECTIONS

Some Gangster Pain: "The Invention of Texas," "The Ancestors Speak," "Dare," "Woman Speaking Inside Film Noir," "Some Gangster Pain," "Suddenly the Graves," "Tonight I Feel Mortal," "Premature Reincarnation."

Tall Stranger: "The Native," "The Birth of a Nation," "The Singer," "Tall Stranger," "The One," "Lee Harvey," "Frontier Days."

Beckon: "My Sister's Hand in Mine," "Beckon," "Standing Still Like Walking, Walking Like Standing Still," "Doubt Sets In," "Lamentation for Martha Graham," "Dorothea Lange," "Heroes, Saints, and Neighbors," "Whose Nocturne," "All Girlhood Receding," "The Birth," "The Big Picture," "3/3/91 4/29/92," "After," "We Don't Have to Share a Fate," "Pale Sojourner."

Lovers in the Used World: "The World (It was just a gas station)," "Several Skylines," "Canon," "Turned Back," "The Sky Drank In," "The Violence," "How Do I," "The World (It is honest)," "The Splendor Fragments," "Childhood Home, a Panorama," "The First Three Minutes," "Lovers in the Used World," "Sapphic: I Said to My Instrument," "Love's Portfolio," "Beauty and the Beast," "Fuck the Millenium," "Flute Girl," "Socrates," "The World (Sweet nullity)," "Date Movie," "The World (Some are born)."

Profane Halo: "Profane Halo," "The River Replaces," "Tincture of Pine," "Sunday Morning," "Native," "New," "The Pox," "Lincolnesque," "This Land Is My Land," "A Little More Red Sun on the Human," "Fatherless Afternoon," "Painterly, Epigean, Dream's Hangover," "Birdman," "One," "The Garden," "My Elected Officials Are Falling into Historical Moments," "Three Figures at the Gates of the Gully," "Burnt City," "Every Epoch," "It Was the Beginning of Joy and the End of Pain."

The Plot Genie: "Culte du Moi," "Schools of Thought," "Romance," "My Name is the Girl with One Glass Eye Said Bitterly," "Brad and Angelina," "Frankenstein," "Shorn Polecat, The Helping Verb for which One Must Keep One's Ears Low," "Do We," "Tyger," "Hitchcock," "Sam Fuller," "Cassavettes," "Tenderness of the Dove," "Paradise," "No One Tells You Like It Is," "Sounds of Freeways Directing the Cosmos Back to its Start."

Peace: "ah oh a sky a fabric an undertow," "Experiments in Patience I," "The Patient," "Experiments in Patience II," "My Mother Moved My Architect," "Experiments in Patience III," "Peace (It fell)," "[Peace] (smells of sweat deep)," "[Peace] (in argument context shivers the trigger words)," [Peace] (contrary to history)," "4th," "[Peace] (death is to be entered backwards)" "Opened," "late democracy," "[Peace] (halftone of a couple in a four-poster)" "[Peace] if a no more one without the other," "Plath and Sexton," "Monday Morning," "Trying to Write a Poem about Gandhi," "Tenderness of the Dove," "Toughness of the Serpent," "A Healing for Little Walter," "A hatchet with which to chop at the frozen seas inside us."

NOTES

"Standing Still Like Walking, Walking Like Standing Still" is for Sarah Provost. "the other side of the screen of your projections" is Luce Irigaray. "no melon patch on a summer's morn" is from Haruki Murakami's *Hard-boiled Wonderland and the End of the World*. "barn place" is Willem de Kooning, from his essay "Content is a Glimpse." Italicized passage in "Date Movie" is a condensation of ideas in Julia Kristeva's essay "Stabat Mater." Sections of "Dorothea Lange" are assembled out of fragments collected from *Dorothea Lange: American Photographs*. "Heroes, Saints and Neighbors" takes its title from a mural by Hawley Hussey and is dedicated to Hawley Hussey. "After " is for Love Nance and Steve Hodges. "Profane Halo" takes its title from Giorgio Agamben. "Fresh hell" is Dorothy Parker. "Tincture of Pine" is for Jeff Clark. "For I have the warmth of the sun within me at night" is Milton. "Lincolnesque" combines material from several speeches and letters of Abraham Lincoln. "Every epoch dreams it has been destroyed by catastrophe" is Theodor Adorno's revision of Jules Michelet's notion that every epoch dreams the one to come. "My Mother Moved My Architect" owes its repetition to Robert Duncan's "My Mother Would Be A Falconress." "Opened" contains phrases from President Barack Obama's speech delivered several days after the death of six people and the shooting of Representative Gabrielle Giffords on January 8, 2011, and radio news phrases following Japan's March 11, 2011 earthquake, tsunami, and meltdown of three nuclear reactors. In "Plath and Sexton" "blue blazer" refers to Sexton's blue jacket bequeathed to poet Maxine Kumin, who mentions it in the line, "the dumb blue blazer of your death" in her poem, "How it is." "A hatchet with which to chop at the frozen seas inside us" is Kafka.

ABOUT THE AUTHOR

Gillian Conoley received the 2017 Shelley Memorial Award for lifetime achievement from the Poetry Society of America. She was also awarded the Jerome J. Shestack Poetry Prize, a National Endowment for the Arts grant, and a Fund for Poetry Award. She is the author of seven previous books, including *PEACE*, an Academy of American Poets Standout Book and a finalist for the Los Angeles Times Book Prize. Conoley's translations of three books by Henri Michaux, *Thousand Times Broken*, appeared in 2014. She is Poet-in-Residence and Professor of English at Sonoma State University where she edits *Volt*.

NIGHTBOAT BOOKS

Nightboat Books, a nonprofit organization, seeks to develop audiences for writers whose work resists convention and transcends boundaries. We publish books rich with poignancy, intelligence, and risk. Please visit nightboat.org to learn about our titles and how you can support our future publications.

The following individuals have supported the publication of this book. We thank them for their generosity and commitment to the mission of Nightboat Books:

Kazim Ali
Anonymous
Jean C. Ballantyne
Photios Giovanis
Amanda Greenberger
Elizabeth Motika
Benjamin Taylor
Peter Waldor
Jerrie Whitfield & Richard Motika

Nightboat Books gratefully acknowledges support from the National Endowment for the Arts and the Topanga Fund, which is dedicated to promoting the arts and literature of California.